People at Work

Working for Yourself

Text and Photographs by Graham Rickard

Titles in the series

Working at an Airport
Working in the Army
Working for a Brewery
Working for British Telecom
Working on a Building Site
Working for a Bus Company
Working for a Chemicals Company
Working in the Civil Service
Working at a Coal Mine
Working in a Department Store
Working for an Electronics Company
Working on a Farm
Working for a Food Company
Working for a Garage
Working in a Hospital
Working in a Hotel
Working for an Insurance Company
Working at a Light Engineering Plant
Working on a Newspaper
Working for an Oil Company
Working for the Police Force
Working at a Port
Working for the Post Office
Working in a Town Hall
Working for Yourself

First published in 1984 by
Wayland (Publishers) Ltd
49 Lansdowne Place, Hove
East Sussex BN3 1HF, England

© Copyright 1984 Wayland (Publishers) Ltd

ISBN 0 85078 455 7

Phototypeset by Kalligraphics Ltd,
Redhill, Surrey
Printed and bound in Great Britain by
R. J. Acford Ltd, Industrial Estate, Chichester, Sussex

Contents

Self-Employment Today 6

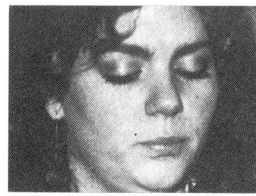
Carol Cruz
Potter
8

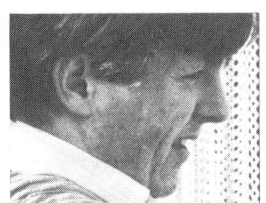
Shaun Morphew
Window cleaner & chimney sweep
13

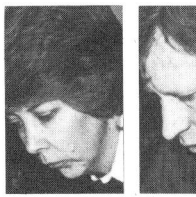
David & Ronda Armitage
Illustrator & writer
18

Jane Heath
Financial adviser
23

Polly Moore
Child-Minder
28

Peter Usher-Wilson
Builder
33

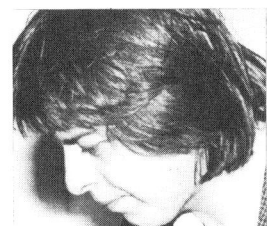
Mike Piggott
Musician
38

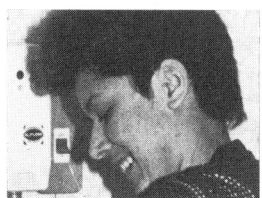
Ismay Wiltshire
Hairdresser
43

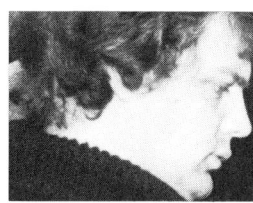
Bob Philpott
Mechanic
48

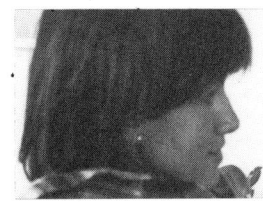
Rosalind Nice
Caterer
53

Edgar Symes
Glass craftsman
58

Mark Burlington
Gardener
63

How to Become Self-Employed 67
Jobs for the Self-Employed 68
Sources of Further Information 68
Index 69

Self-Employment Today

There are many free pamphlets giving advice to anyone who wants to set up their own business.

The self-employed now make up about 10 per cent of Britain's total working population of 26.5 million – and that percentage has been rising during the last few years of increasing unemployment. Many professional people, including doctors, dentists and solicitors, are self-employed; but there are thousands of others, working either on their own or with a small work-force, who have set up their own businesses, supplying a wide range of goods, services and skills.

Many skilled workers, especially in the building and construction industry, operate mainly on a self-employed basis, although they are in fact employed by someone else. These jobs, such as bricklaying and labouring, are often advertised in Jobcentres, and in the 'Situations Vacant' columns of local newspapers.

Today, there are self-employed people doing every conceivable kind of job, from making pottery to cleaning drains. Some of them are involved in traditional trades and crafts, but the new technologies are also offering many opportunities to the self-employed – as program writers for computer software, for example.

Most people in Britain are happy to be employed by someone else. They enjoy a high level of job security, a guaranteed wage every week or month of the year, paid holidays, sick leave, and a company pension when they finish their working life. So why do so many people sacrifice these benefits to take on the risks of being self-employed? There is no easy answer. People become self-employed for a variety of reasons. Some, who have found it impossible to find a job, have no choice – they are faced with self-employment or unemployment, and opt to do the best they can, with whatever skills they have.

Others, disliking the routine and restrictions of working for someone else, decide to become self-employed to gain more freedom to choose what to do with their time, or perhaps to follow their special interests in life. They are more than willing to exchange security for freedom.

Most people, at some time in their working lives, think of becoming self-employed or setting up their own business. But, whatever their reasons for doing so, it can be a difficult and confusing step. Careful thought is necessary before taking the plunge, and several legal requirements should be taken into consideration.

With determination and hard work, however, it can be a very satisfying way of earning a living, and there are many individuals and organizations who can offer help and advice to anyone thinking of setting up their own business (see page 68).

The unemployed still outnumber the self-employed by about one million, but the government is trying to reverse that position by the introduction of the Youth Training Scheme and the Enterprise Allowance Scheme, which is specifically designed to aid new, self-employed businesses.

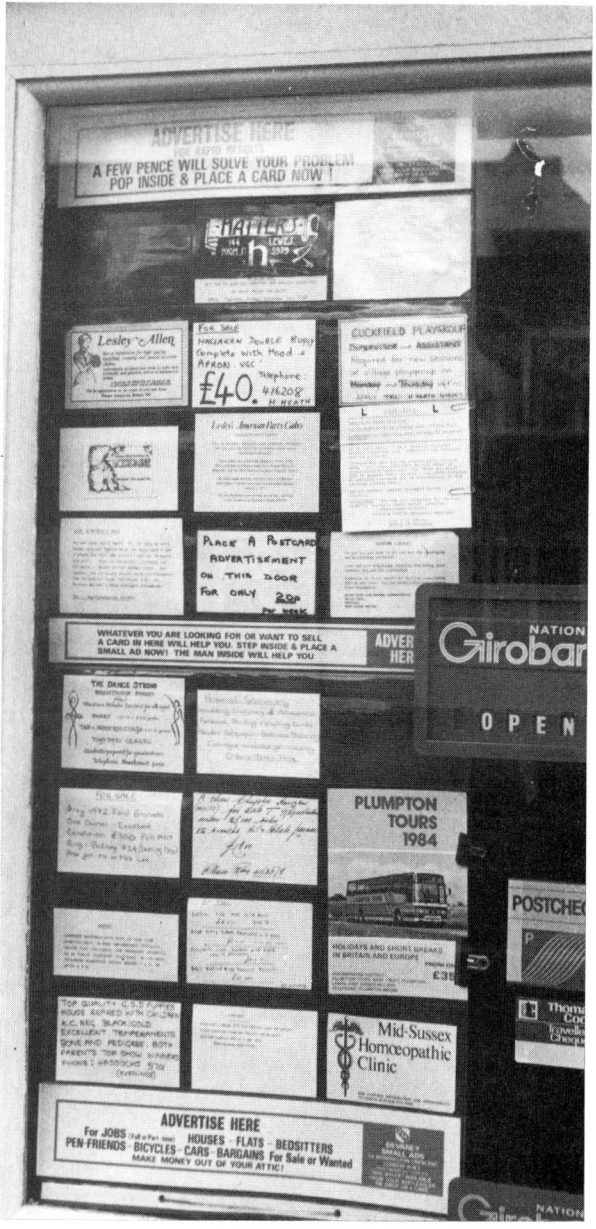

Putting cards in shop windows is a cheap and effective way of advertising your services.

Carol Cruz
Potter

Carol Cruz is 19 years old and has just set up her own pottery workshop. She was unemployed when she decided to apply for the new Enterprise Allowance Scheme. Under this scheme a person setting up their own business is guaranteed a wage of £40 per week for the first year, provided he or she has £1,000 to invest in the business.

Since I was a little girl, I've always enjoyed crafts, such as enamelling and modelling clay, and I first tried pottery at school when I was 11. Ever since then I've always wanted to be a potter, running my own business. But I had no money, and nowhere to set up a studio, and the situation seemed hopeless until I heard of the Enterprise Allowance Scheme.

I went to a comprehensive school near Crawley, and left when I was 16, with 5 CSEs and 2 'O' levels in art and pottery. I then went to Crawley College of Technology for two years to do a City and Guilds Arts and Crafts Diploma course. I also passed another pottery 'O' level, which was more on the theoretical side of the craft. It was a very busy two years, but I enjoyed it.

When I left, I couldn't see any way of becoming a potter without any financial backing and, to earn some money, I moved to Bognor Regis to work as a receptionist in a cinema. I enjoyed the experience but the pay was poor, and it was very difficult to save any money. I left after three months, moved back home and started looking for premises to rent as a workshop.

I was unemployed at the time, and my future prospects looked pretty bleak, until I read about the new Enterprise Allowance Scheme (EAS) in the local paper. The very next day I went to the Jobcentre to make enquiries, and they got in touch with the local EAS office to arrange an appointment. One of the conditions of the scheme is that you have at least £1,000 to invest in the business, which could have been a problem. But after talking things over with my Dad, he was good enough to lend me the money. He's done the same for my brother, who's also on the Enterprise Allowance Scheme.

I filled in an application form, and went to the EAS office. There I was asked if I'd been employed for the necessary time of thirteen weeks, and they wanted to be sure that I was not being helped by anyone else. They seemed quite interested in my work, agreed to accept me, and I signed all the papers. During my first year of trading, I'm guaranteed an Enterprise Allowance of £40 a week, on top of any profit I make.

Carol checks the quantities of materials in one of her pottery reference books.

The EAS local office keeps a check on the progress of your business, and I have to inform it if I'm ill, but I'm allowed a paid holiday. The scheme has been very helpful – in fact, there's no way I could have started without it, because all my initial profits will be ploughed straight back into the business. The EAS office also put me in touch with the Small Firms Service, which gives advice and publishes a whole range of very useful leaflets for people in my position.

My brother and I went to see the bank manager with our £1,000 cheques, and both opened a business account. He was very friendly and helpful, and when the business has taken off I'll be able to approach him for an overdraft or a loan to cover the cost of any extra equipment. My £40 weekly allowance will be paid directly into my account every fortnight, and I can use the account to pay for my National Insurance stamps by direct debit every month. From the account, I'll pay myself a set weekly wage to cover bills, material costs, and also all my personal living expenses.

This pottery pencil case was one of Carol's early experimental projects.

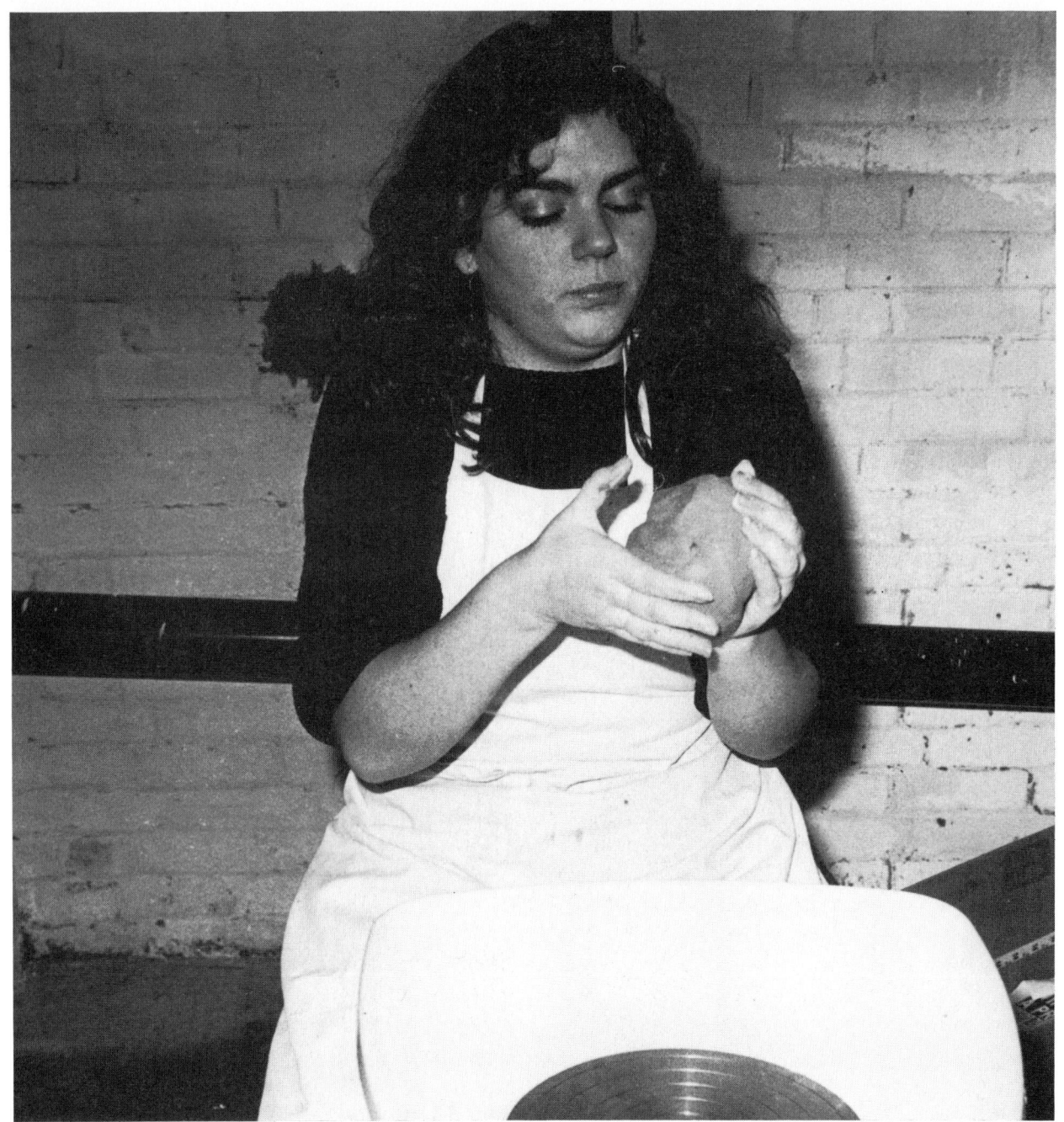

My brother and I also went to have a chat with our Dad's accountant, and he told us how to keep our books and issue receipts and invoices, and he agreed to look after our tax affairs. It's very important to have a good accountant, because he knows exactly what you can claim as tax-allowable expenses from

Carol rolls a lump of clay into a ball before putting it on the wheel.

receipts for equipment, materials, petrol and other outgoings. Unfortunately, the £40 allowance is taxable.

It was very frustrating looking for working premises, because every time I thought I had found a suitable place, it all fell through. My father is self-employed as a maker of fishing tackle, and my brother was about to set up in injection-moulded plastics, so we decided to look for a place together. We eventually found a 400 square-foot workshop unit on a private industrial estate, and set to work renovating and decorating it.

There is enough space for the three of us to work together without getting in each other's way. We've shared the costs, which were much higher than we expected and we'll be able to share travelling expenses from home. We've installed heating and lighting, and we'll have a cooker, kettle and radio, so it should be a real home from home!

I've sold some of my pottery in the past. I shall be making mainly functional domestic items, such as teapots, cups, plates and ashtrays. I have all my designs and colours drawn up on paper, and will spend the first few weeks making up a complete range of samples to show to potential customers. There are a lot of craft shops in this area, and the few that I've already approached have shown an interest, but they obviously want to see my work before placing firm orders. My faithful old Morris 1000 estate car will come in useful for deliveries and collecting materials, and we'll have a telephone in the workshop for taking customers' orders. I already have some orders from friends and relatives.

I'm having some business cards printed, to leave with shopkeepers. Apart from making personal approaches to craft shops, I'm going to try an unusual sales technique – 'pottery parties', held in people's houses (like Tupperware parties) where groups of friends can see and buy my work at reduced prices. There aren't many potters around here and, as I

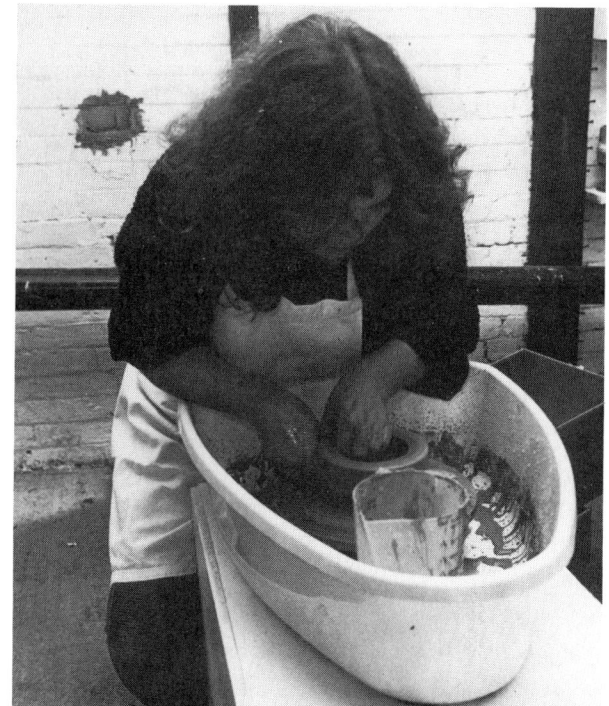

Above *In Carol's skillful hands, a pot begins to take shape on the wheel.*

Below *The finished products – Carol takes a jug and a mug out of her kiln, after it has cooled down.*

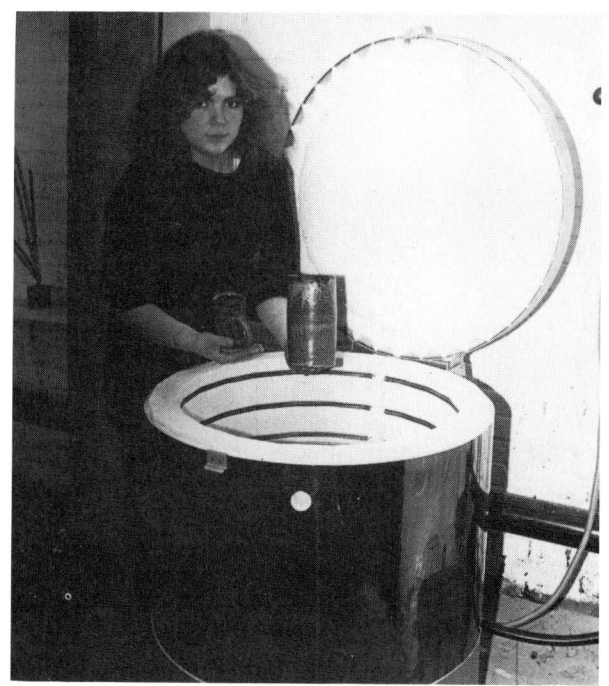

shall be covering quite a wide area, including several large towns, I'm hoping for good sales. Once the business has settled down, and I'm more experienced and confident, I shall try approaching the larger department stores, such as Habitat, Harrods and Liberty's.

When I first decided to set up on my own, I didn't realize half of what is involved, but I've had plenty of encouragement from people who've seen my work, and all the advice I've had has been very useful. There isn't much change left from Dad's £1,000. My kiln alone cost nearly £800, and I've had to buy a wheel, clay, glazes and various finishing tools. I only have enough clay to make my samples, so replacing it will be a big expense when I get my first orders. I buy all my materials from a specialist firm in London, and collect them myself to save the delivery charge.

Carol screws a light-bulb fitting into one of her stoneware lamps bases.

I won't be able to base my prices on an hourly labour rate, because my products would be too expensive. I have to be competitive if I hope to sell. The £40 a week will come in very handy until I become organized and can work quickly. I'll base my prices on what others are charging, but I'll have to be careful to cover my costs – there's no point in working hard just to lose money.

I've never been keen on working for other people, and I'm really looking forward to selling my own work, and my own designs. I know that I'll have to work long hours, and be very self-disciplined. I've always loved going out a lot, and playing badminton and tennis, but I won't have time now. Optimism and enthusiasm are necessary at this stage, because it would be very easy to worry too much about the future. But I'm glad I've taken the plunge, and I refuse to even contemplate failure – I've always hated losing at anything!

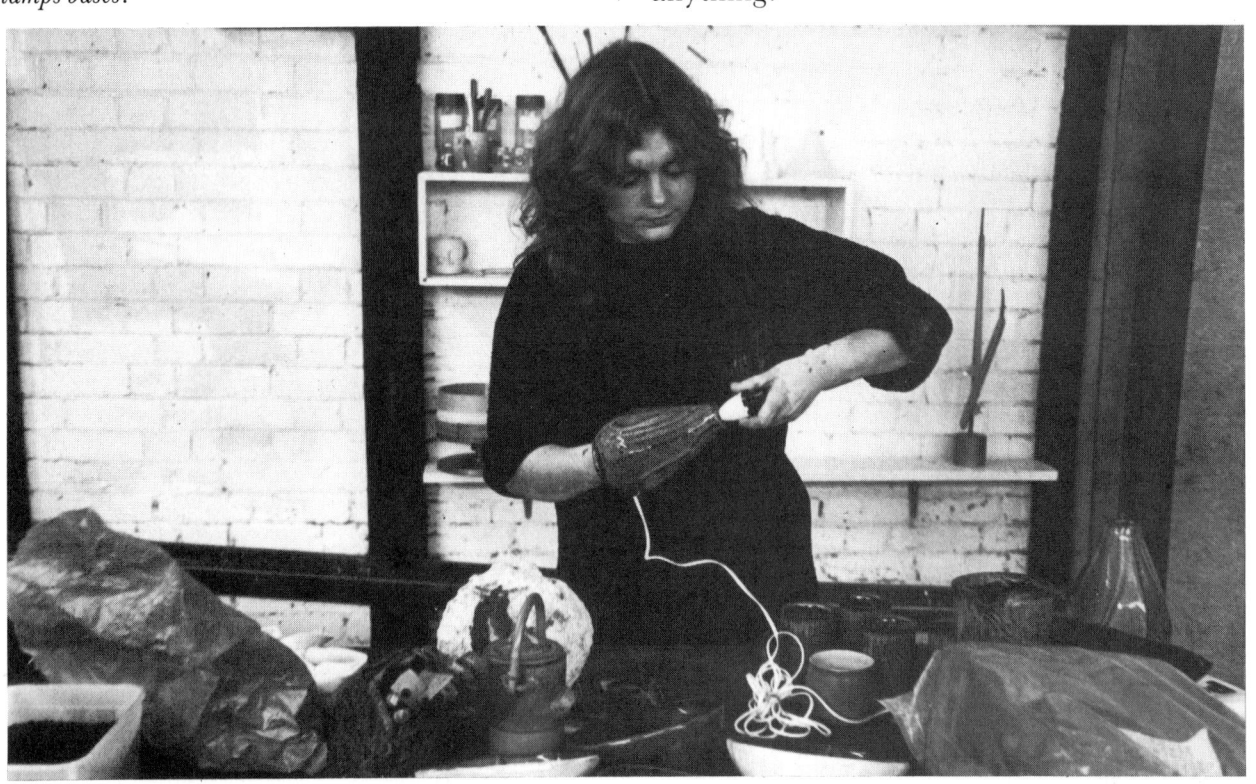

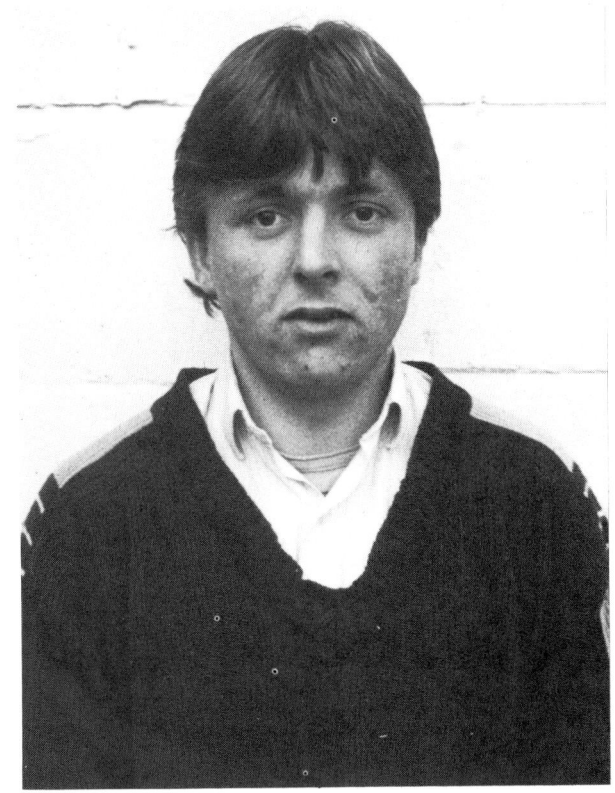

Shaun Morphew

Window cleaner and chimney sweep

As a committed Jehovah's Witness, Shaun Morphew wanted a job which would provide him with a living wage, and still leave time for the religious activities which play such an important part in his life. Still only 18 years old, he earns enough to support himself by working two days a week as a window cleaner and chimney sweep.

I became self-employed out of necessity. Because I'm an active Jehovah's Witness, I needed a job with flexible hours, so that I could have plenty of free time for our door-to-door visits and other religious activities. I was brought up as a Witness and, since the age of 16, my religious interests have played an increasingly important part in my life.

I went to a comprehensive school, and left when I was 16, with 1 CSE and 7 'O' levels. My grades were good enough to take 'A' levels, but I wasn't too keen on school and didn't want to stay on for the extra two years.

My Dad is a bricklayer, and I worked in the building trade for a while after leaving school before I decided to become self-employed.

I had already done a little window cleaning with some friends and knew that it was easy to drum up work which paid well if you work hard, needed little capital outlay, and had flexible hours. So, at the beginning of 1983, I bought my ladders, buckets and scrims (cleaning cloths). Then it was a matter of walking around local streets, knocking on doors and canvassing for business. After seeing their windows, I gave people a price on the spot, and cleaned them there and then, which meant I was earning while finding my first customers. It was a fairly easy business to set up. The car was my biggest expense; the rest of the equipment was about £100.

The business took off quite quickly, and was well established within three months. I started working two days a week, covering a fairly wide area. For someone without transport, though, it's possible to do the job on foot, concentrating on a small area: a friend of mine makes a good living from cleaning the windows on one large housing estate. I found that word of mouth was the best form of advertising; sometimes I started with just a couple of houses, and soon found myself regularly cleaning the windows of almost the whole street.

In mid-1983 I decided to branch out into chimney sweeping, which can't be done on the same sort of shoe-string budget. I borrowed £500 from a friend to set up the business because an industrial vacuum cleaner costs £250, and I had to buy rods and brushes – and public liability insurance became essential too. I had some handbills printed and put them through most doors in local towns and villages. They cost me £15 per thousand (which is cheap, because I have friends in the printing business) and proved to be a good long-term investment. The response was slow at first, because people tended to put away the bills until they needed their chimneys swept, but business gradually picked up.

I decided to try chimney sweeping because I was getting fed up with cleaning windows all the time, and wanted to start a new venture which could eventually take over from the first. I want to move on in life, and not spend the rest of my days cleaning windows. I prefer cleaning chimneys because there's more to the job, and more day-to-day variation. As well as being better paid, I get to know and talk to the customers much more, and it's something I can do even when the weather is bad. It's not steady work, because people tend to forget about their chimneys until they want to use them at the beginning of winter, but it balances well with window cleaning at the moment.

Before I started, I already knew a little about chimneys and flues from my work on building sites, but apart from that I just picked it up as I went along. Window cleaning still provides most of my work, but I'm building up my sweeping equipment, and I hope that chimneys will soon be providing most of my income.

To make the most of each working day, I get up early and have a large breakfast, so that I don't have to stop for lunch. I wash out the

The start of another day's work.

scrims, load the car with my buckets and ladders, and drive to my first job. I have a contract to clean the windows of show houses on a housing estate, and I start these at 7.15 a.m. in summer. I visit my private customers once every five weeks, and I usually make a start on these at 8.30. Depending on the size of the houses, I cover about fifteen customers a day, and my fee varies between £2 and £20. At first I used to charge 25p per medium-sized window, but when I became more experienced, I based my charges on a labour-rate of £6 per hour. That sounds a lot, but I don't want to have to rush, and I have to take travelling time into account. I charge about £10 an hour for sweeping chimneys, depending on how difficult the job is.

After washing a window, Shaun cleans it with a squeegee.

For cleaning windows, I first use a lamb's wool applicator with a mixture of water and washing-up liquid. Then I clean it off with a rubber-bladed squeegee before finishing with a damp scrim. First-time customers sometimes have very grimy windows which take longer to clean, so I charge them a little extra for my first visit.

Before starting to sweep a chimney, I remove everything from the area, clean out the fireplace, and remove the grate. I tape a blanket over the fireplace and lay a dust sheet on the floor – I try to work as cleanly as possible, because no one wants soot all over their carpet. After putting the vacuum tube in the grate, I screw the first rod on to the brush and and start to sweep the chimney. I keep adding more and more rods until the brush sticks out the top of the chimney. It can be very hard work, especially if the chimney has a sharp

Luckily, Shaun has no fear of heights, although he doesn't like cleaning leaded windows like these.

bend. You also have to remember to keep twisting the rods in the right direction, otherwise they'll come loose and get stuck half-way up. When I've finished, I always clean up any mess, and take the soot home to tip into a large hole in our back garden.

I always ask clients to remove any valuable objects, but I did once smash an ornament on a mantelpiece. The owner said it was worth £150, but I had noticed that it was already damaged, and he eventually agreed to forget about it if I swept his chimney for free. That's why public liability insurance is essential for any chimney sweep. My policy only costs £30 a year: not a lot to pay for peace of mind!

I found it difficult to talk to people at first, especially when it came to asking for money. But I'm used to it now, and my work as a Jehovah's Witness has helped me to get on better with customers.

I finish work early in the evening, and I usually have some fish and chips or a Chinese take-away if I feel too tired to cook. I share a house with two other lads, who are both self-employed, so my rent is fairly low. When I get

Shaun screws on more rods until the brush clears the top of the chimney that he is sweeping.

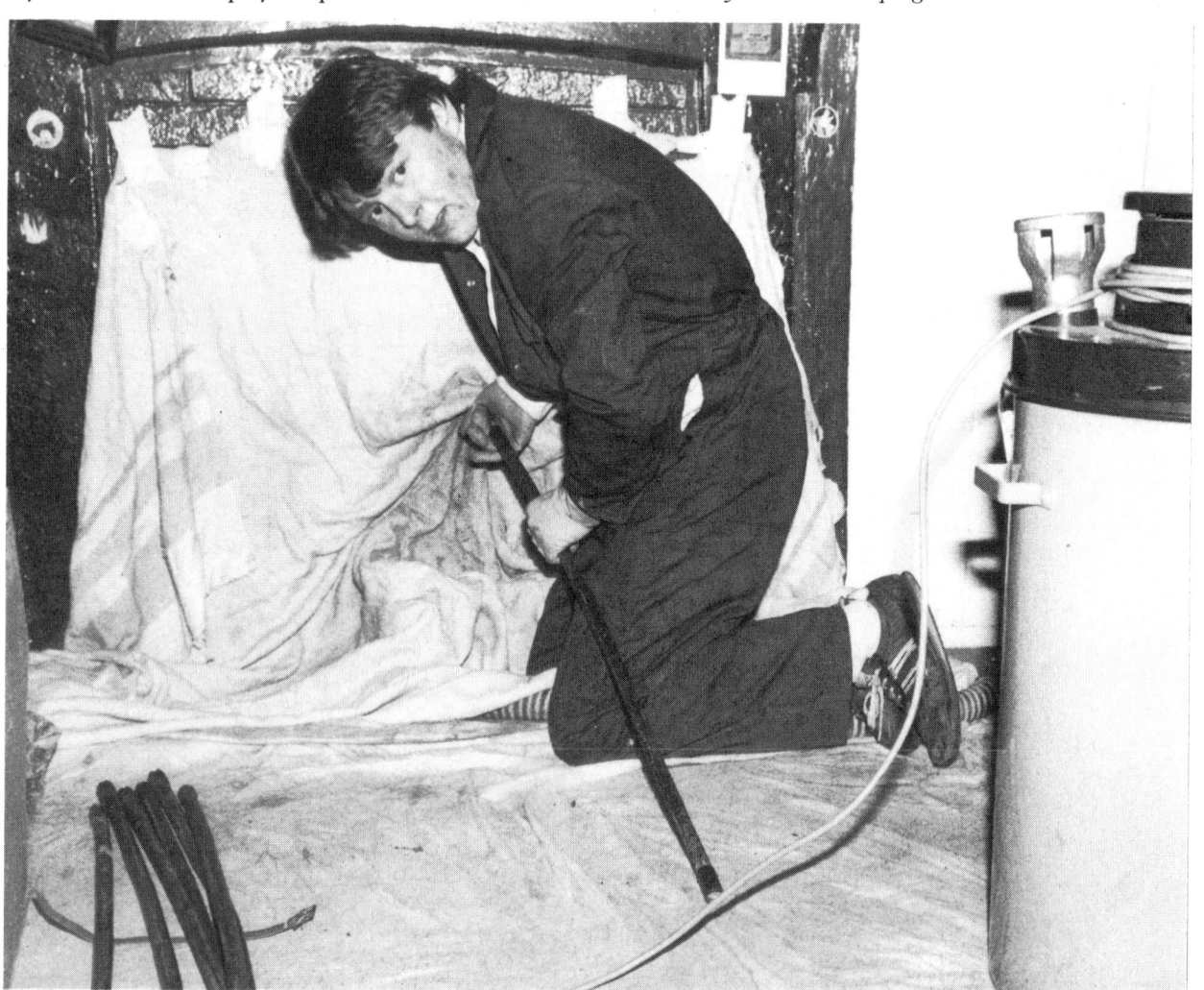

home, I listen to any messages on the telephone-answering machine, and follow them up with a few telephone calls. We all depend to a certain extent on the telephone for our business, and we share the cost of the machine. Sometimes customers aren't in during the day when I clean their windows, so I have to go back in the evening to collect my money. I never have any problems with collecting payment, and working just two days a week provides enough money, about £70 per week, to keep me going. The car is my biggest expense, because I drive at least 250 miles every week.

I buy all my materials for window cleaning and chimney sweeping from specialist suppliers. I have two friends who are window cleaners, and every four months we share the cost of a trip to Kingston, near London, to replace such items as scrims and rubber squeegee-blades. Because we are in business, we get a trade discount, which makes the trip well worthwhile.

As I'm paid in cash, I have a building society account, and manage without a bank account. I keep a careful record of my income and expenses, and it takes me a couple of

Shaun removes the loose soot after cleaning the chimney.

The indispensable telephone. A customer makes an appointment with Shaun to have his chimney swept.

evenings at the end of each financial year to balance my books. I want to handle my own tax affairs if possible, but I'm still not sure what items I can claim as tax-allowable business expenses.

Anyone who wants to become self-employed should think carefully about the work, speak to as many people as possible who are in the same line of business, and work out the cost of a bare minimum of equipment. Debts cause extra pressure, so it's best to manage without a loan if you can. It's essential from the very start to keep careful records of your income and outgoings, and to take your work seriously – it's your reputation which will decide whether you fail or succeed at your job.

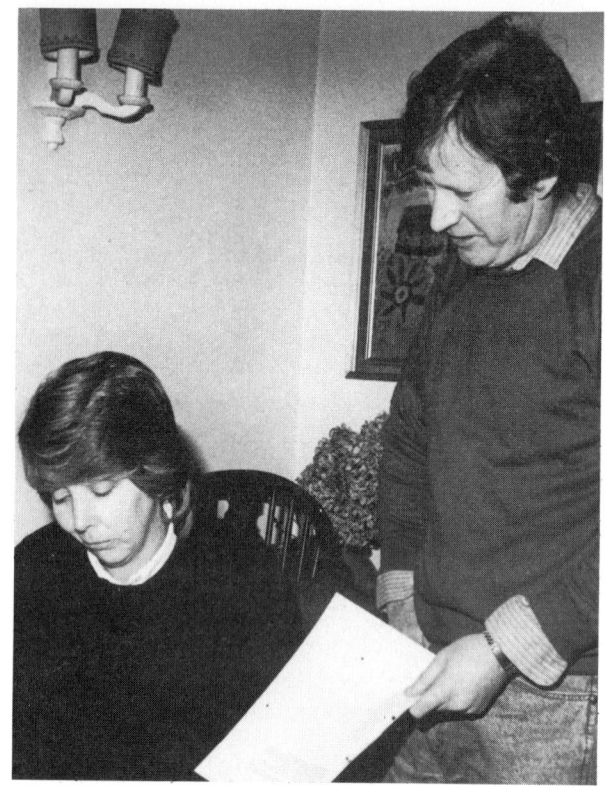

David & Ronda Armitage
Illustrator and writer

David and Ronda Armitage, both 40 years old, are a successful husband and wife team, producing colourful books for young children. Ronda writes the stories, while David illustrates and designs the books. Here, David explains how their partnership works.

Even when I was a child, I was always drawing. While I was studying for my school exams in Australia (where I was born and brought up), I took drawing lessons at night school, before going on to take my diploma in fine arts at a polytechnic. Ronda's story is similar. She grew up in New Zealand, and as a child used to amuse herself by writing stories about sheep-rustlers! She went to university before becoming a teacher, and then worked in a children's bookshop before starting to write stories herself.

I was painting theatre scenery for a living and Ronda was a teacher when we both decided to give up our jobs and come to England. We didn't know each other then, and met on the boat journey. Neither of us had a clue what we were going to do. After a succession of odd jobs, we travelled around Europe and Russia in a battered old car, before returning to New Zealand where I organized exhibitions at the Auckland Art Gallery. My own paintings began to sell well. We had two small children by then, so we decided to travel again before they were old enough to go to school. We came back to England, intending to stay only a couple of years – that was eleven years ago, and we're still here!

The first few years were very difficult, because I was trying to break into the design market in London's publishing world. After a couple of years scratching around for work, I realized that there were more opportunities on the illustration side, so I concentrated on it. I eventually met an editor who suggested that I should find a good text, and present it to a publisher as a complete package, including illustrations and design. I couldn't find a suitable text, so Ronda said she'd write one for me! She came up with a good story, called *The Lighthouse Keeper's Lunch*, and we had great fun working on it together. It was the first book she'd ever written, and the first that I'd ever illustrated, so it was put together in a fairly haphazard way. We didn't know then the conventional way of doing things, which I think is part of the secret which lies behind the book's appeal.

Having completed the book, we then had to persuade someone to publish it. The first two publishers turned it down, and we were beginning to feel depressed when I gave it to André Deutsch. When Ronda drove home on Christmas Eve, I had pinned a huge canvas on the garage door, with the message, 'Yes, they've taken it, and they want more, more, more!' It was a marvellous Christmas present, and we haven't really looked back since then. It proved to be a very successful book, and has been reprinted eight times. It's also been sold to foreign publishers, and was one of two of our stories to be presented on BBC TV's 'Playschool' programme.

That book was a real breakthrough, because it made a name for us, and established my reputation as an illustrator and designer. We've just finished our eighth book together, and we usually try to bring out one a year.

Ronda and David look through their latest book.

Below *Ronda helps David to sort through his illustrations, as they try to choose some for an exhibition in London.*

David does the finishing touches to an illustration for his and Ronda's new book.

When we start on a new book, we talk over our ideas for a while, until we have a rough story-line. We work to a 32-page format, so the next step is to put the outline of the text on a story-board. I draw out some 'dummies' for the illustrations, trying to find visual personalities to fit the characters, while Ronda fills in the details of the story. We work together fairly well, although we do have the occasional argument, usually if Ronda thinks that my illustrations don't match the text!

We submit a rough outline, with a few finished illustrations, to the publisher for approval before continuing. Since our first book, we've always used the same publisher, partly out of gratitude for giving us our first break. Other publishers do sometimes approach us, but we both have plenty of work, and don't really have time to produce more than about one book a year. It could also lead to a problem of over-production, and the books might lose their appeal as we ran out of original and imaginative ideas.

Apart from our books, I do a wide range of freelance work, mainly illustrating and designing books for publishers. I generally handle all the design details of a book, from the artwork on the front cover down to the typeface to be used in the text. I usually accept the work as a complete package, which makes life easier for editors, and any specialized work – such as photography – is then 'farmed out' to experts. I have a wide range of contacts in every field of art and design who can produce high standards of work.

I sometimes paint portraits. I also teach art at a local evening class, and design newspaper adverts for local shops. I'm still very much involved with my own paintings, although I try to keep that as separate as possible from my commercial work.

Ronda also has several different interests apart from our books. She works one morning a week in the local Citizen's Advice Bureau, and helps out at a nearby primary school. She's taking a course in counselling at Brighton Polytechnic at the moment. When I'm very busy she often helps me with my work. We receive many invitations from schools and organizations to give talks about children's books, which is something we both enjoy doing.

I enjoy the variety of my job. I often do as many as five or six different things in one day. Most of my commercial work is done in a rented studio, which I share with two other people. I'm having a new studio built outside our house. When I'm not in the studio, I spend a lot of time visiting publishers, delivering and collecting work and discussing new projects.

I enjoy the freedom of freelancing and being self-employed, but there is a price to pay: because of the insecurity of the work, I find it very hard to say 'No' to any job, and I often end up working all weekend to meet a deadline. Ronda also enjoys the freedom and variety of our life style. She used to find that full-time teaching was very demanding, and didn't leave her with enough time to live her own life, and follow up her interests.

We are paid royalties on our book sales of 10 per cent of what the publisher earns from them, which we receive twice a year. With a new book, we are given an advance on our royalties. We also receive payments when a book is sold to a foreign publisher; when a hardback book is sold to a paperback publisher; and when one of our books is used on TV. Under a new scheme, we are also paid a Public Lending Right, a sum of money based on the number of times readers have borrowed our books from public libraries. In this way our books continue to provide a source of income long after they were first published.

With my freelance work, I'm sometimes offered a price for a job on a 'take it or leave it' basis, but otherwise I estimate my fee according to the time it takes and the cost of materials. I charge more for illustrations than for designing a book because it needs more originality. It usually takes three months before I'm paid by a publisher.

When not doing illustrations for children's books, David likes to do abstract paintings, like this one hanging on the wall of his lounge.

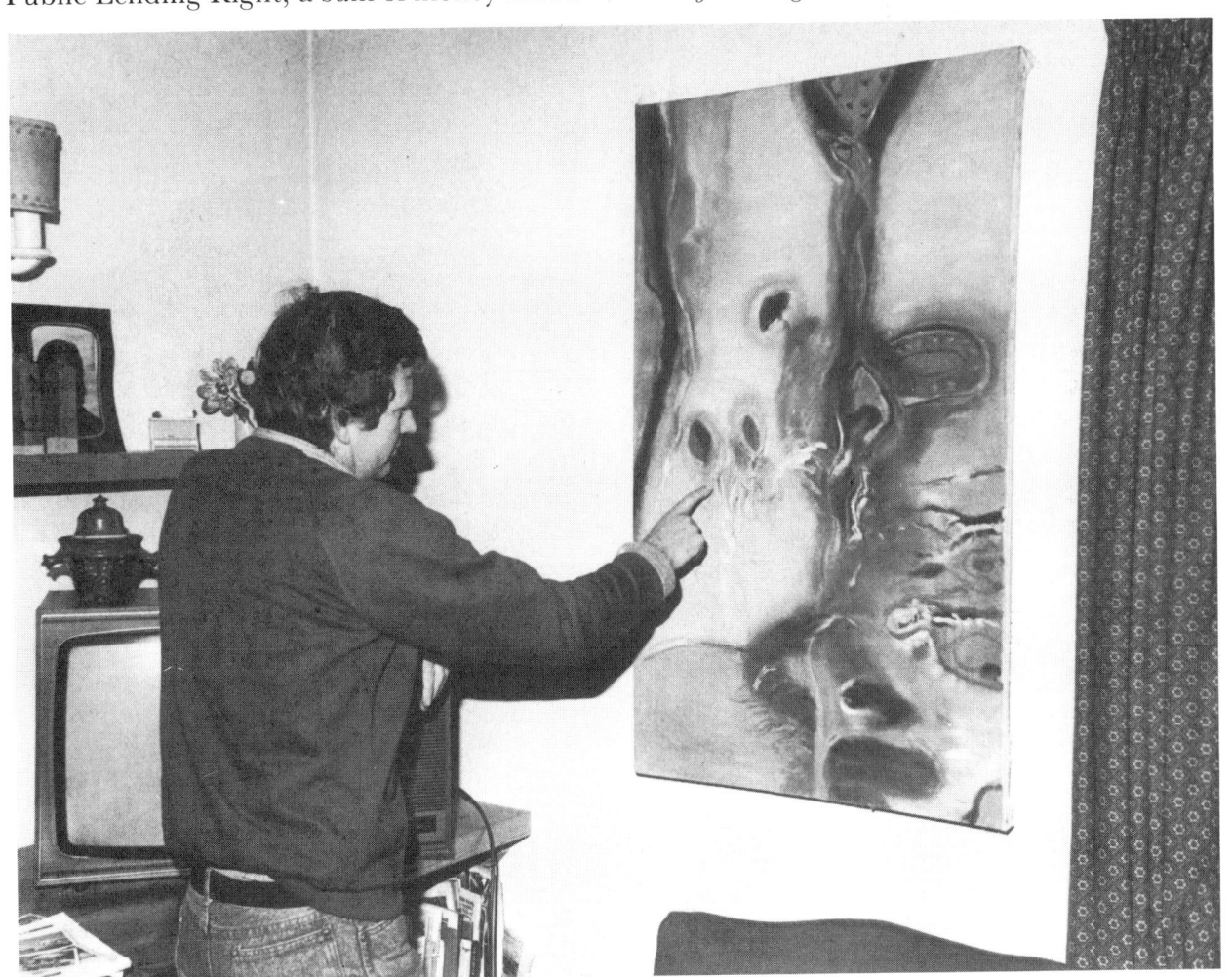

Ronda and I have a joint business account, and each month we both transfer a set amount into our separate private accounts. We have an overdraft facility at the bank, which is very useful for overcoming life's little cash-flow problems, and an accountant works out our twice-yearly tax payments. Because we have a fairly high annual turnover, we are VAT registered, and we have to make our payments every three months. I charge an extra 15 per cent to cover this, and I claim back any VAT which I have paid during the year. It's a very complicated form of taxation, involving a lot of paperwork.

I have a health insurance policy to provide us with an income if I'm taken ill, a pension scheme, and life insurance. My car and equipment are also insured, and I'm covered for public liability, although that's not really necessary in my line of business.

Ronda agrees over the phone to give a talk to a local school, and makes a note in her diary.

I always try to give clients a good service, and keep in contact with every aspect of the publishing world. Apart from my reputation and good name, most of my work comes from personal contacts. It's not much use being the best artist in the world if the phone never rings.

It's very easy to fall into the trap of never taking a holiday. Travelling is very important to both of us, and we make a point of going abroad for a break as often as we can. It's good to broaden your experience with as many influences as possible. In our case, I think it stimulates our imaginations, and improves our work. One day, we'd like to produce a book from beginning to end, even publishing it ourselves – now that would be fun!

Jane Heath
Financial adviser

Jane Heath is a financial adviser. Although she works for a company of investment and insurance brokers, she is self-employed on a commission basis. Aged 23, Jane has to choose the best personal finance plan for each of her clients.

I'm a very sociable person and I've always been interested in financial matters and working with figures, so this job suits me down to the ground! I value my independence, and being self-employed means I'm running my own business within a business. My job is very important to me, and it's up to me to make the best of it. I can't blame anyone else for failures and I get all the credit for good work.

I have a very wide range of clients – including company directors, book editors and building labourers. I especially like dealing with self-employed people, because they do such a variety of jobs, and their needs and circumstances can be very unusual. They usually have no pension, no sick pay or holiday pay, so I can nearly always help them in some way. I genuinely care about my clients, and always do what's best for them, rather than making the highest possible commission for myself. It's very satisfying being able to help people who often don't really understand money-matters – especially the young and the self-employed.

I live at home with my family, who aren't involved in finance, apart from my stepfather, who's an accountant. I left the local comprehensive when I was 16, with 5 CSEs and 4 'O' levels, including maths and English. I then moved to a sixth form college to take 'A' levels in English, biology and geology, but I felt that the teachers were treating me like a child, and I left after the first year.

Chemistry was always one of my favourite subjects, and I decided that I wanted to be a public health inspector, one of the few jobs which combines chemistry with meeting the public. But there were no vacancies at the time, so I started applying for jobs which I saw advertised in the local Press or at the Jobcentre. After a few weeks, Brighton Council interviewed me and offered me a post as a trainee accountant, dealing with mortgages. I had to wait three months before starting the job, so I filled in the time by working as a temporary clerical assistant with an agency.

When I started work with the Council, I did a day-release course in accountancy at Brighton Polytechnic, but I never finished it because I left the job. I then worked in London for two years as a tax assistant with a firm of accountants, and started on a course for tax inspectors. The job held no hopes of promotion, though, and again I left before finishing the course.

I had managed to save some money, so I decided to travel around Europe. After working in West Germany and Greece, I went to the USA for a year before returning home.

For some time I had wanted to be a financial broker, working with both people and figures, but it's usually a very difficult field for a female to enter. In the Jobcentre, Reid Trevena and Co. Ltd., a London-based firm of investment and insurance consultants, were advertising for brokers, and I arranged an

Jane begins her day by phoning up potential clients on her list of referrals.

Jane shares an office with two other advisers.

interview with them. In the initial interview, they questioned me about my financial position, my experience, and why I wanted the job. They were obviously interested in me, and in their second interview their concern was also whether I felt capable of doing the work, and had enough initial contacts to start the ball rolling. They interviewed me as if I were a prospective client, and gave me a sales presentation to learn.

A week later, I went back and conducted a sales interview with a manager. I was accepted, mainly I think, on the strength of my out-going personality; I try to be cheerful and friendly, and showed that I could be confident in dealing with people. A few days later, I went to our London head office for a one-week intensive introductory course to the world of insurance and investment broking.

I started working for Reid Trevena in 1983, and, even with full management support, it was down to my own efforts. I had to generate my own work and see it through. I started by approaching people I already knew, and business took off very well but it slowed down as soon as I ran out of contacts. It was my own fault because I didn't ask my clients for 'referrals' – other possible clients who they

Jane has just organized a personal finance scheme for this garage owner and his partner.

Below *Jane's car is very important as she travels hundreds of miles each week to meet her clients.*

knew – and I was left with no potential clients to approach. I had to work a lot harder and start from scratch to rebuild my business, but I won't make that mistake again! Luckily my business built up again, and now it's going well, but I have to make new contacts all the time to succeed in the job.

I work with a group of about twenty other brokers, based in an office in Brighton. We have full managerial support to guide us along both in and out of the office, and the company provides a receptionist and telephones for our use. The telephone is very important, because that's how I usually make my first contact with potential clients. I arrange a preliminary meeting with them, which is just an informal chat, and I fill out a questionnaire about their personal finances. I try to find out what they want from life, assess what they can afford to save, and decide whether I can help them in any way.

Everyone's needs and circumstances vary, and after this initial meeting, I go back to the office to work out the best possible financial plan for each client. We represent most of the leading financial institutions in the country, so there is a wide range of plans to choose from. I handle every kind of insurance policy, including car, life, health and public liability, as well as pension schemes, investment plans and bonds.

When working out the various premiums, I take into account the client's age, state of health and personal circumstances. I arrange a second meeting, when we can conclude any business. I have quite a high success rate, as about 50 per cent of my initial contacts eventually become clients. They also give me the names of other people who may be interested in my services – these are the all-important 'referrals' which I rely on. I see my clients every six months to check that their needs haven't changed.

Jane has her own drawer in the office filing cabinet, where she keeps all her clients' details.

I'm usually in the Brighton office by 8.30 a.m. to sort out my paperwork and arrange the day's work. I start by phoning my referrals, in order to make some appointments. I'm usually on the phone for at least an hour – both a telephone and a car are essential for this job. Then I usually sort out some queries, obtain a few quotes from insurance companies and finish my paperwork before driving to my first appointment. Each one usually lasts about an hour, and I often don't have time for lunch. After three or four meetings, I drive back to the office to make yet more telephone calls before going home for dinner. Most evenings, I have a couple of clients to see, because many people aren't free to see me in the day.

On the office wall is a personal progress chart, showing the weekly sales of each adviser.

A good telephone manner is a real asset in this job, and it's important that you are smartly dressed too, because it inspires confidence when you are handling people's financial affairs. I also have to be discrete in handling confidential information about clients. Luckily, I have a very good memory for faces and names, which is a great help if I bump into a client in the street, or meet one several months after my first contact with them.

I'm paid a commission on each plan I recommend. The commission differs according to the policy, and my monthly income still varies quite wildly, because I'm not consistent enough. Basically, the harder I work, the more I earn, and I'm now doing fairly well. In fact, I've become one of my own clients, and sold myself a savings plan with built-in life assurance!

I pay my National Insurance contribution monthly, by direct debit from my bank account. I also do my own book-keeping, filing records of my expenditure on petrol, car repairs, telephone bills and stationery, and my stepfather handles my tax affairs.

Anyone thinking of becoming self-employed should research their market, find enough capital to last for the difficult first few months and make as many contacts as possible. One essential quality is determination and stamina to see you through problems. We have a saying in our business: 'When the going gets tough, the tough get going!'

Polly Moore
Child-Minder

Polly Moore, 29, loves children, which is fortunate, because she spends her whole day surrounded by them. As well as her own three children, she looks after four others. She started child-minding almost by accident. But now she is very involved in her work, and sits on the local child-minders' committee.

I'm certainly not a 'career woman'. When I left school all I wanted to do was to get married and have children. I was one of ten children, so I'm used to being surrounded by kids, and I enjoy their company. But I never really considered child-minding as a job until a friend suggested that I should try it. I already had three young children of my own but I decided to give it a try. I've been looking after other people's children for the last two years and I really enjoy it. While the children are with me they're part of my family. I've also become very involved with the local child-minding organization in Brighton, which has given me an extra interest in life.

I left secondary modern school at 15, with no qualifications and no idea of what I wanted to do. At first, I worked as a shop-assistant in British Home Stores and Sainsbury's, but I had no real interest in the work – it was just a job, with no personal involvement. Then I worked in a chemist's for a while, which was more interesting because I was put in charge when the owner was away. I was offered a permanent job as manageress, but I turned it down.

After I married, I was quite content to be a housewife, looking after my three children. But a friend, who was a child-minder, was asked to look after more children than she could cope with, and she suggested I should become a child-minder. After talking it over with my husband, Roy, I decided to register myself as one with the local Social Services Committee. Then I had to attend a couple of meetings, and the police provided reports on Roy and myself to ensure that we had no records of child abuse or other crimes. Our doctor's records were checked for contagious illnesses, and the fire department visited our house to check the safety standards.

Although it wasn't compulsory, I attended an eight-week course on child-minding,

Polly is never happier than when she is surrounded by children.

which covered play, first-aid, how to detect signs of child abuse, and several other topics. It was useful because it taught me what to expect from the children, and what they should expect from me.

The quality of service provided by child-minders varies quite a lot, and not all of them are registered. It's quite easy to register, and I think it's a good idea for anyone who is thinking of becoming one. Now and again, a lady officer from the Social Services Department calls to check on my standards, but I see her quite often anyway, because I'm now on the local committee of the Child-Minding Association. I also edit our newsletter, and advise new members on what the job entails. I also run *Touchline*, which is a list of local child-minders with vacancies for children. I update it every three months. I find that it's a very good way of putting parents in touch with competent and registered child-minders.

Parents need child-minders for different reasons. Sometimes a student may become pregnant in the middle of a college course which she wants to finish; while others, especially one-parent families, have to work to make ends meet. The Social Services occasionally pay us to look after a problem child when the parents need a break because they just can't cope.

I'm allowed to look after four children. I started with one, and enjoyed it from the very start. I found it very easy to be a 'professional parent' because I was already so used to children, and I take a real interest in them. Some children, can be real 'horrors' at home, but they're usually very good with me – my only problem is my own children! I've never found discipline a real problem, and I only smack children when they're very naughty. Raising my voice is usually enough, although kids usually 'try it on' when they first come to me, just to see how far they can go.

While they're here, I'm responsible for bringing them up, and I treat them as if they were my own children. I have to feed them, keep them clean and warm, and help them to develop until they are old enough to go to nursery school. I play and talk with them as much as possible, and Roy and my own children help to keep them entertained and happy. I'm lucky that Roy is as fond of children as I am, because he often helps me out.

The parents bring the children each morning and collect them in the evening, and I usually look after them for about ten hours each day. Once a year, the local child-minders give the children a free outing. Last year we took 35 kids and 10 adults to a zoo-park. We almost ended up with an extra child, because my husband rounded up a little boy who had nothing to do with our party!

Polly reads the children a story.

My day starts at 7.00 a.m. when I do the day's washing; the little ones need clean nappies, and I always keep a complete change of clothes for each child, so there is always plenty of washing to do. Roy makes breakfast for us before he goes to work, and the first two children arrive at 7.30. They come with me when I take our sons to school, and I do the shopping or pop in to see a friend on the way home. The second two children arrive at 9.30, and they amuse themselves while I start preparing lunch. Some of the smaller children attend a local playschool twice a week in the mornings, so I have to collect them before giving all the children their lunch.

Then it's nappy-changing time, and the very young ones have a sleep in the afternoon. The others usually play with the toys, or the clothes which I keep for dressing-up. Two go to nursery school in the afternoon, and I often take the others to the park until school finishes at 3.00. We usually have an early tea, and I make a cake if it's someone's birthday. After tidying the toys away, I read to them and they watch their favourite TV programmes until their parents collect them. My day isn't finished when they leave, though; I cook my husband's tea, do the washing up, and put the children to bed before I can relax.

Polly's husband, Roy, helps out by wiping the children's faces when they have finished their tea.

It sounds a very hectic day, and it can be very noisy with so many children around, but I love it. I can organize my time as I want, and it can be quite challenging, teaching kids how to behave, how to eat, and how to treat others. I've looked after 6-week-old babies and 4 year olds. I have them for varying amounts of time, from a few months to several years.

I occasionally have to tell parents tactfully when their children aren't suitably clothed, or need new shoes, which can be difficult. I sometimes miss the children when they leave, usually to go to school, especially if I have had

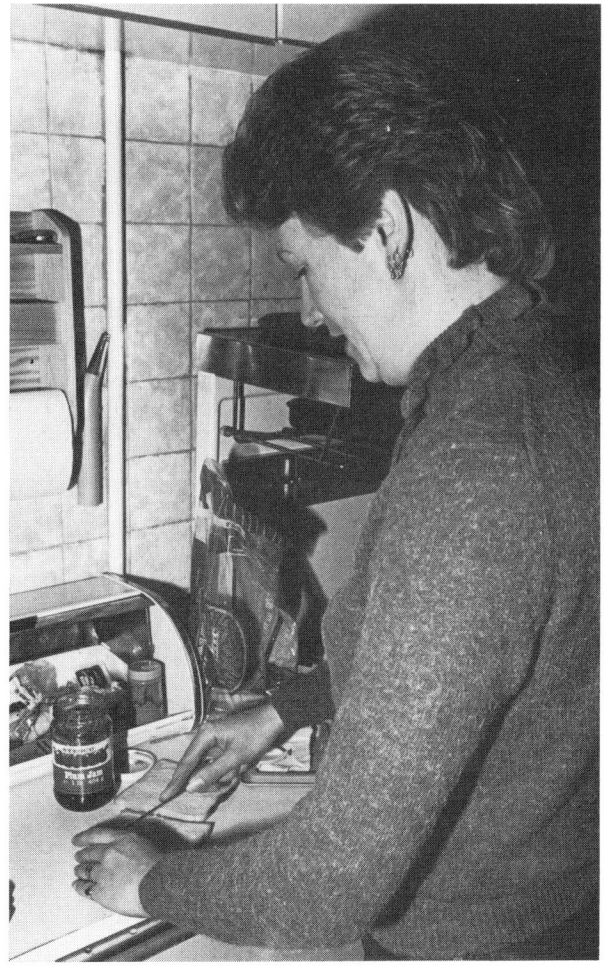

Polly makes the sandwiches for the children's tea. She makes a cake if it's someone's birthday.

Over the phone, Polly puts a parent in touch with a registered child-minder who has vacancies.

them for a long time. One day, I wouldn't mind working in a children's home, but at the moment I just take each day as it comes, and I don't really have any plans for the future.

The National Child-Minders' Association recommends standard rates, but it's up to the individual to charge what parents can afford to pay – obviously single-parent families, for example, can't afford very much. I charge a daily rate of 65p an hour, or a yearly rate which works out a lot cheaper. In addition to my time, I have to provide high chairs, cots, pushchairs, nappies, potties and all the other essential items. I use the telephone a lot to get in touch with parents, and my gas and electricity bills are high, so I don't think I'll ever make a fortune from child-minding!

I'm covered by Roy's National Insurance contributions, and I don't have to pay tax because I earn less than the married women's allowance of £1,875. Before I started, I had to take out a special child-minder's public liability insurance policy, which covers any damage which the children might cause.

I've never had to advertise and most parents hear of me through friends. When they come to me, I ask them to fill in a form with the child's personal details, so that I know of any medical or dietary problems. They also sign an agreement which sets out the terms and conditions of my employment.

Sickness can be a problem, because one child with a contagious illness, such as conjunctivitis or diarrhoea, can infect all the others, so I sometimes have to ask parents to take their children home if they have such an illness. Otherwise, problems are few and far between, and I've never regretted the day that I decided to register as a child-minder.

Polly says goodbye to one of the children as her mother comes to collect her.

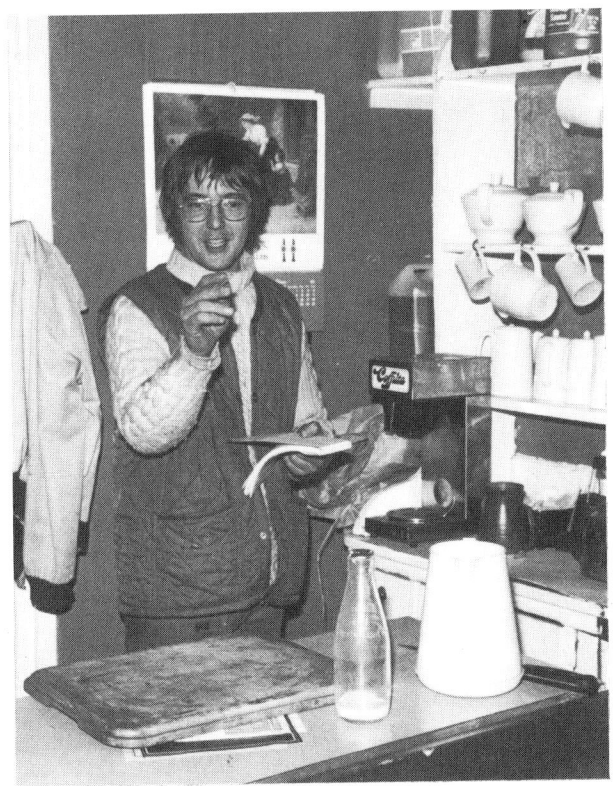

Peter Usher-Wilson
Builder

Peter Usher-Wilson, 29, is a very practical person, trying his hand at several different jobs before he set up his own building and property maintenance business in 1980. He found the first year difficult, as he had to learn all the different trades and do the work himself; but he now farms out some of the jobs to sub-contractors.

I've had no real practical training in the building trade, but I used to do building and maintenance work on my parents' farm, and during school holidays I worked as a labourer on building sites. I went to a local grammar school, which I left when I was 18, with 6 'O' levels and 3 'A' levels, including maths and engineering. I started a degree course in engineering at Hatfield Polytechnic, but I didn't enjoy it, and my level of maths wasn't up to scratch, so I left after eighteen months. After working as a milkman for nine months, I went to Leicester Polytechnic, where I completed a diploma course in estate management. After a short spell as a pipe-layer, I worked for an estate agent for four months, valuing and selling hotels, guest-houses and rest homes.

That was my last professional job really, and during the next few years I tried my hand at all sorts of jobs, in Britain and abroad.

Then I decided to start up my own building business. I had no real training, and little experience, but I felt that it was something I could start with a minimal capital outlay. I already had most of the basic tools, and I bought my materials as I needed them, sometimes with the help of a bank overdraft. I started with painting, repairing gutters, and small carpentry jobs, and picked up the various skills as I went along. I didn't advertise, and I sometimes found myself short of work. During these slack periods, I used to fill in with car maintenance, van-driving and casual work to help make ends meet, but the business steadily improved.

I think the business took off because I always turned up when asked, accepted even the small uneconomical jobs which others would have turned down, was reasonably priced, and I never cut corners. I always take a pride in my workmanship, and this has paid off, because I now have a good reputation,

Above *Peter collects all the materials and tools that he will need for the day's work.*

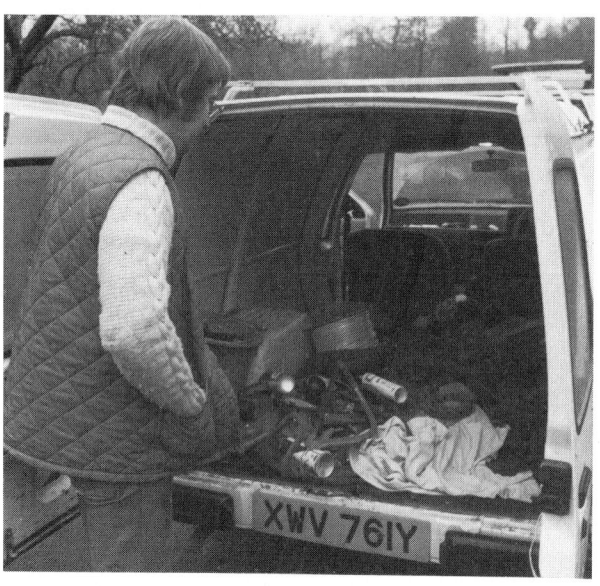

A quick check that he has loaded everything that he needs into his van, and then Peter is off to visit one of the sites where people are working for him.

and most of my business comes through word of mouth, from previous satisfied customers. I'm now very busy, and I've moved into a semi-management position, because I sub-contract a lot of the skilled work. It's cheaper for me to employ specialist labour, rather than trying to be good at everything myself.

Under the Youth Training Scheme, I also employ Graham, a 16-year-old school-leaver. Over the next year, he will come to me for five or six months of on-site training in painting and decorating. The rest of his time will be spent studying his trade at a local technical college.

Now that I employ outside labour for skilled work, I can have several jobs 'on the go' at one time. I spend most of the day supervising the work and keeping everything running smoothly. I'm also responsible for estimating new work, buying materials, handling customers, organizing my business finances, and dealing with local government planning departments. But I still enjoy the practical side of the work – in fact, I quite often end up working as a labourer for the skilled staff on my own sites!

Most days, I get up before 7 a.m., have a light breakfast, and make out a list of tools and materials for the day's work. After loading the van, I drive to the first site, which could be a house extension, for example. I organize the work-force, find out what materials they need, and start them working. I have a credit account at a local builders' merchant where I buy most of my materials, at trade discount. When you're buying materials all the time, it's much easier to pay for it all on a monthly account.

After delivering the material, which could be anything from cement to roofing-felt or plumbing fittings, I usually tidy up the site, or help with the labouring by carrying bricks or mixing cement. Most mornings I have to see some customers, or deal with the various officials involved in the building trade, including architects, planning officers, and building controllers. There are many rules and regulations which have to be complied with, and all sites are regularly inspected.

Before the morning is over, there's usually time to visit a second site to check the progress of the work and sort out any problems. I don't usually have time for a proper lunch-break, so I just eat a couple of sandwiches.

In the afternoon, I often go to the bank to pay in customers' cheques and to withdraw cash from the business account to pay my work-force. I then have a second tour around the sites, and check they're all left clean and tidy at the end of the day. I'm usually the last to leave the site, after arranging the next day's work programme. After supper, the telephone often starts ringing as customers ask me for estimates on various jobs. I usually spend an hour each evening phoning people, writing estimates, and checking my expenditure and income.

I don't like having to chase people for my money. When customers don't pay up on time, I have to pay the bank interest on loans and overdrafts, which eats away at my profits. Customers sometimes expect me to wait a lot longer for my money than they would be prepared to wait for their wages! I always pay my debts promptly, and I wish they would do the same. Sometimes I have to waste my time advising clients about a job when they obviously can't afford the work, which can be very

Peter helps his apprentice, Graham, to strip the wallpaper in a house he is renovating.

A local hotel-owner and his wife tell Peter of their plans to move their kitchen into another room. They would like Peter to do the job for them.

frustrating, because time is money. I'm not very keen on doing my paperwork – such as VAT returns and invoices – but now my accountant handles most of that for me.

In the future, I'd like to move into property development and renovation, buying and selling houses myself. This kind of business pays well, but needs more capital. The bank should be able to help me, because I've proved to them over the past few years that I can do the work, and that I can handle my financial affairs responsibly.

I buy my National Insurance stamps on a monthly basis, with a standing order from my bank. Its manager is fairly understanding and helps me with any cash-flow problems, so that I can pay my suppliers while waiting for customers' cheques. I have a good accountant, which is essential, and he earns his fee several times over in tax savings and financial advice.

My annual turnover is pretty high, but I also have very heavy expenses to consider, before seeing what is left as a profit. Labour and materials are both very expensive, and my transport costs are quite high as well.

I am a member of the National Federation of Self-Employed, which costs me £70 a year. I consider it money well spent, as a form of professional insurance. They would help me if anything went wrong, by offering free legal advice if I was sued by a customer, and representing me in VAT appeals. I also have several insurance policies, including public liability, employer's liability, a pension fund, and vehicle and accident insurance. One policy came in very useful recently when I slipped off a ladder, fell through a conservatory roof, and injured my back and an eye. During the two and a half months that I was off work, the insurance company paid me a weekly sum to keep me going – otherwise I would have been in trouble. Accidents can happen to anyone, however careful and safety-conscious, and it's wise to prepare for the unexpected.

I find my work challenging, and being self-employed suits me because I don't like working for other people. If I work hard, I reap the benefits myself, instead of lining someone else's pockets. I earn more than I could by working for someone else, but I also work a lot harder. I enjoy my independence, and it's really satisfying seeing a semi-derelict property turn into a smart, comfortable home. The results of my work are usually very visible and easily appreciated, both by myself and the customer.

Some degree of experience is essential for anyone thinking of setting up in the building trade. To start on a small scale, £500 would probably buy the necessary tools and some form of transport. A practical nature, self-confidence, and the discipline to work when you don't really feel like it are also necessary. You need to be able to get on with people, including customers and bank managers, and able to keep a careful check on money – otherwise it's very easy to come away from a job with nothing to show for it.

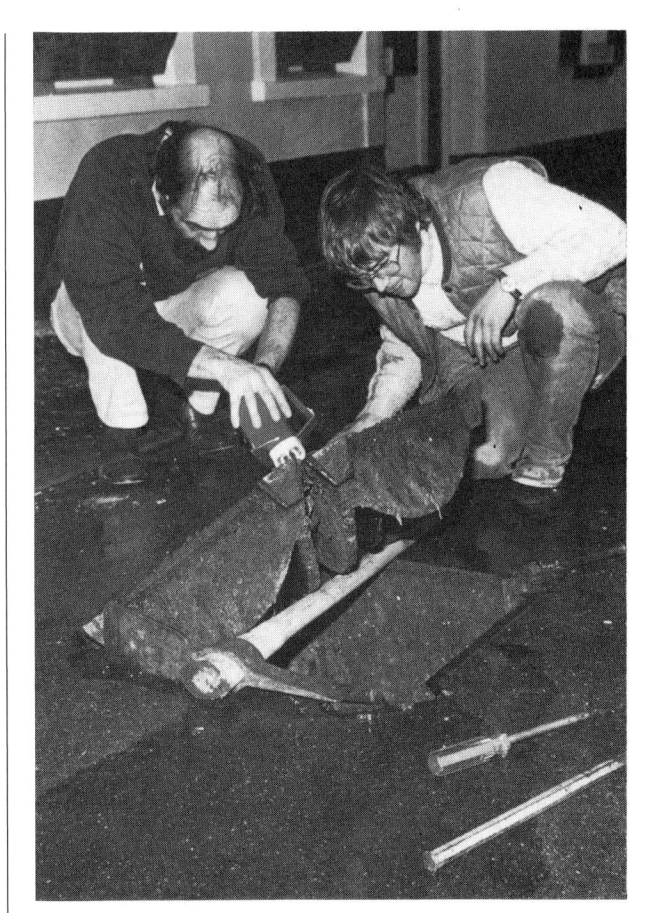

Above *Peter and the hotel-owner inspect the drains to see if moving the kitchen will create drainage problems.*

Below *Peter checks a planning application for an extension to a house against the architect's plans.*

Mike Piggott
Musician

Mike Piggott is 35 years old, and has been a professional freelance musician since 1968. He plays several instruments, and many styles of music, and is in constant demand for concerts, tours, recording sessions, and radio and TV appearances. His more unusual bookings have included Prince Andrew's 21st birthday party, and playing the violin in an exploding orchestra for a 'Pink Panther' film.

Music isn't only my job, it's my whole life really, and I've never wanted to do anything else. People tend to think that musicians are all wealthy superstars, living lazy and luxurious lives, but it's a false image. I'm a hard-working regular musician. Sometimes, it's true, I can earn up to £180 in a single day, but such days can be few and far between, because there's no security in this business, and the bad times can soon drain away the money I've made in the good times.

Apart from my grandmother, who played the piano, no one in our family was musically inclined, and I had no real interest until I was asked at school if I wanted to learn an instrument. I was only 9 years old, and I chose the violin purely because I knew two little girls in our street who used to play it! Before I started playing in my first rock band, I only played classical music, and I was made leader of the school orchestra.

I've always been grateful for my basic classical training, especially being taught how to read music, because it's an essential skill for any serious professional musician. 'Pop' musicians can sometimes get by without being able to read a single note, but I'd never have got anywhere if I hadn't been able to read music. At some recording sessions, for example, I only have an hour or so to go through the music before going into the studio to record!

I went to a public school in Ramsgate, where I started studying for three 'A' levels, after passing 5 subjects at 'O' level. But then I became involved with my first rock band, which played gigs several nights a week, and I left school at 17, before taking my exams.

The band didn't earn enough to live on, so I had to start looking for a job. A friend from school was working for the BBC in their tape library, so I wrote to him, asking to be shown around. The work seemed interesting, and I

Mike is a very versatile musician, playing several different instruments.

liked the idea of working on the production side of broadcasting, so I asked for an interview. I was offered a job in the tape library at Broadcasting House, and I worked there for two years.

I did a course in book-keeping and typing, and my prospects with the BBC looked pretty good, but I was still playing in the band. Because of all the late nights, the situation became impossible, and my boss told me that I had to make a choice.

Our band had plenty of work at the time, so I quit my job and decided to devote myself to music full time. Looking back on it, it was probably a bad decision, because the work dwindled to a trickle, and I didn't have enough experience or contacts. I applied to the BBC again, and was accepted, but I had to start right back at the bottom of the ladder, so I left yet again.

While building up my contacts and musical skills, I used to take on all sorts of fill-in jobs, including hospital portering, to help pay the bills. But gradually I was offered more bookings with various bands, and things started to look up. I still work a few mornings each week in a local music shop, restringing violin bows. It pays fairly well, but I also enjoy it, and I now have enough work as a musician not to have to look for casual work.

I play five or six nights each week, in concert halls, clubs and pubs, with half-a-dozen bands. They all play different styles of music.

I've recently joined the Pentangle, a re-formed folk band, and I've got great hopes for our future. We've already recorded an album.

During the day, I'm sometimes booked as a session musician for records, or TV or radio programmes. I'm a member of the Musicians' Union, which lays down standard rates for this work – usually about £45 per three-hour session. It's essential to join the union, and membership isn't expensive: it costs me about £30 a year. It's well worth it, because the Union protects my rights, and even collects my royalties for certain jobs. I receive my royalty payments twice a year, but no royalties are payable if you're paid the standard recording fee for a job.

Above *In a recording studio, Mike reads music and wears headphones to listen to the backing track.*

Below *Mike plays his guitar with a jazz-rock band.*

In a folk club, Mike plays traditional tunes on a mandolin.

Because there is no security in this business, my income varies considerably from week to week. Some work, such as recording, pays very well, while pubs and clubs are still paying their musicians the same money as they did ten years ago. In fact, on a really bad day, you might not get paid at all! Last summer, for example, I played three separate performances at an open-air folk festival, and was paid £10, which didn't even cover my petrol expenses. I'd previously agreed a fair sum with the festival's organizers, and I'm now taking the case to the Small Claims Court in the hope of getting some more money.

On several mornings a week, Mike works at a local music shop, mending violin bows.

Instruments and amplifiers can be very expensive when you first start, but after that a car and petrol are the main expenses. I travel about 20,000 miles a year in my car, and that doesn't include journeys by rail or air. I often travel abroad, and I've played in just about every country in Europe and Scandinavia, although I haven't yet been to America. Strings can also be expensive; I change my guitar strings after two or three gigs, and a set of good violin strings costs up to £14.

I used to try advertising for work in the *Melody Maker*, but it wasn't really worth it, usually because the work I got wasn't suited to my taste or personal style. Nearly all my work comes as the result of a phone call from a personal contact. When people ask me how to become a session musician, I find it very hard to answer. I may be a good musician, but even if I were the best in the world, I would be lost without this network of contacts in the business.

It's hard work, too, and not nearly so glamorous as people imagine. They imagine that we all sit around in plush hotels drinking champagne, but the reality is usually a cup of tea at 3.00 a.m. in a transport café on a motorway! I often don't get home until the early hours, and the constant travelling does get tiring. It doesn't leave much time for family life, either, so I usually try to leave some weekends free, to spend with my four children. Constant practise is essential to keep your fingers supple and to improve your technique. I should practise at least three hours a day, but I just don't get the time.

But I love playing music, especially with other people, and I'm now in the lucky position of being able to organize my own life, and only accept the work I want to do. I'd like to have a more steady flow of work and income, to make myself more financially secure, but I'm full of hope for the future now that my band, the Pentangle, have had such a good response from our first few bookings.

I make a note of what I earn, and of my expenditure on such things as travel, equipment, stage clothes and instruments. I sort it all out once a year, and take it to my accountant, who looks after my tax affairs. I buy my National Insurance stamps every week, and I have a life assurance policy, as well as insurance policies to cover my car and valuable instruments.

There aren't nearly as many places to play now as when I first started. Some have closed, while others have gone over to disco music rather than live bands, so it's much harder for young musicans to get any solid gigging experience. I made the mistake of leaving the job at the BBC too early, but at least I gained plenty of experience. If a young person feels that they have the talent and stamina, then they should go ahead and not let anyone put them off, but it's best to gain some experience and build up professional contacts before jumping in at the deep end.

Wearing a dinner suit, Mike tunes his violin before playing for a charity ball at the Dorchester Hotel in London.

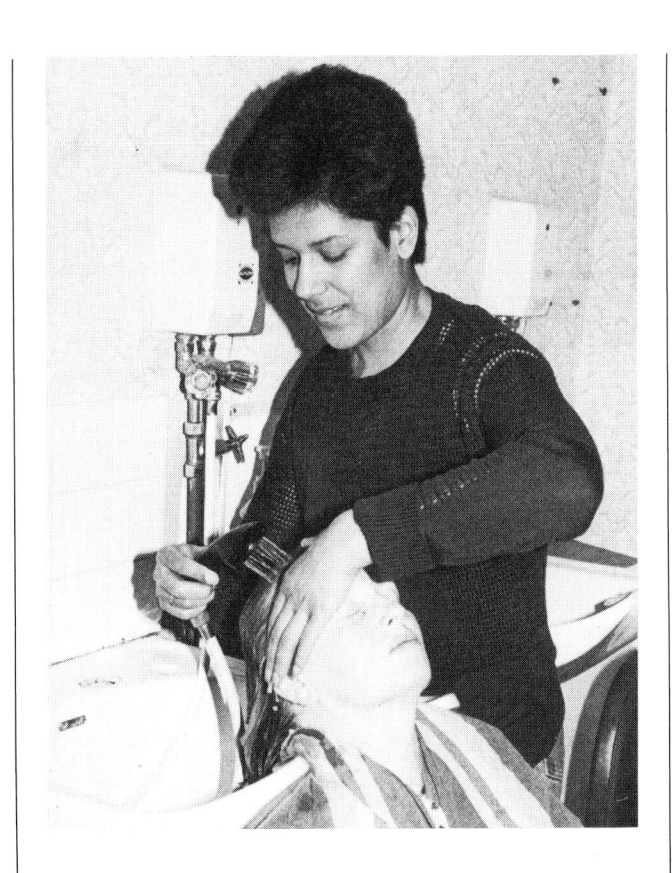

Ismay Wiltshire
Hairdresser

Ismay Wiltshire, 25, has been running her own hair salon in a Sussex village for three years, and her appointments book is nearly always full. She was lucky to take over an existing business. She found it hard work at first, but the salon now runs smoothly.

When I was a little girl, I used to cut my dolls' hair. I've always wanted to be a hairdresser, ever since I was at primary school. I don't know why, because there were no other hairdressers in the family.

I went to a comprehensive school, and left when I was 16 with 5 CSEs, which is plenty for this job. I then did a two-year full-time City and Guilds hairdressing course at Crawley Technical College. When I became self-employed I did a one-year course at evening classes in running a business, which has since proved very useful because it taught me how to handle the money and keep my books straight.

I applied for my first hairdressing job before leaving college, and was accepted immediately. I enjoyed the work from the start, because I was finally doing what I had wanted to do for years. Unfortunately it didn't last long, because the business closed down. I worked in two or three other salons after that, gradually building up my skills and experience. I was given each job I applied for, because my employers were always pleased with my work and gave me good references.

I was working here with the previous owner of the salon when the lease came up for renewal. She decided not to renew it, and asked if I'd like to take over the business. I had already run the salon while the owner had been away on holiday and enjoyed it, so I was very pleased to be given the chance to take it over. In return for an agreed sum, I bought all the equipment, furniture and fittings. So, unlike most people who start up on their own, I began with an established business.

I was very busy from the start, and I worked very hard in the first year. Now things have eased off, although I have a steady flow of business. On most days, I'm fully booked from 9 a.m. till 1 p.m., and 2 till 7 p.m. Two local schoolgirls help me out in the evenings

Ismay stands proudly outside her salon in a small village in East Sussex.

and on Saturdays. I give them a proper training, although they're not interested in going into hairdressing.

Before opening the doors at 9 a.m., I clean and tidy the salon, and prepare for the first customer. I spend an average of half an hour with each one. I do a wide range of work each day, including shampoos, sets, perms, cuts, tints and blow drying. I think this is a skilled job, needing a certain amount of artistic flair.

The work sometimes needs organizing carefully, to avoid wasting time and keeping customers waiting too long. While I'm cutting one person's hair, I might have up to three others sitting under the driers. I have quite a few male customers, most of whom just want a straight cut, but some have a shampoo and set. Most of my regular customers are from

Ismay adjusts the drier while one of her customers settles down with a book.

the surrounding towns and villages, although a few do come from farther afield. Women tend to regard having their hair done as something of a social event, and look forward to it. So I try to keep the salon clean, bright and cheerful and make their visit as enjoyable as possible. I'm always friendly towards them, and give them the kind of personal service which they wouldn't find in the large salons.

It's important to be able to get on well with people, and I spend most of the day chatting to them as I do their hair. Some are very fussy, but you have to remember that 'the customer is always right' – and my business depends on satisfying my customers. A rude hairdresser would soon go bankrupt!

A specialist dealer in hairdressing supplies calls here once a fortnight to take my order for materials. I receive them a few days later – shampoo, setting lotion, towels, curlers, scissors and anything else I may need. The quality is always good, and it's cheaper to buy materials direct from a trade dealer. He also keeps me informed of all the new products which are constantly coming on to the market. To keep up with all the latest styles, techniques and products, I also read three or four hairdressing magazines.

Customers pay me before they leave the shop, so I don't have any problems in collecting my money. Most people also give me a tip, usually between 10p and £1, although it can be as much as £5 at Christmas. This extra money comes in useful for personal luxuries, and even those who don't tip often give me cakes and sweets!

I have a lot of bookwork to do, which is the worst part of my job. I keep account of the daily takings and all outgoings, and check the petty cash, which is mainly used for giving change. I make a note of what I pay my part-time girls, and any cheques have to be paid into the bank.

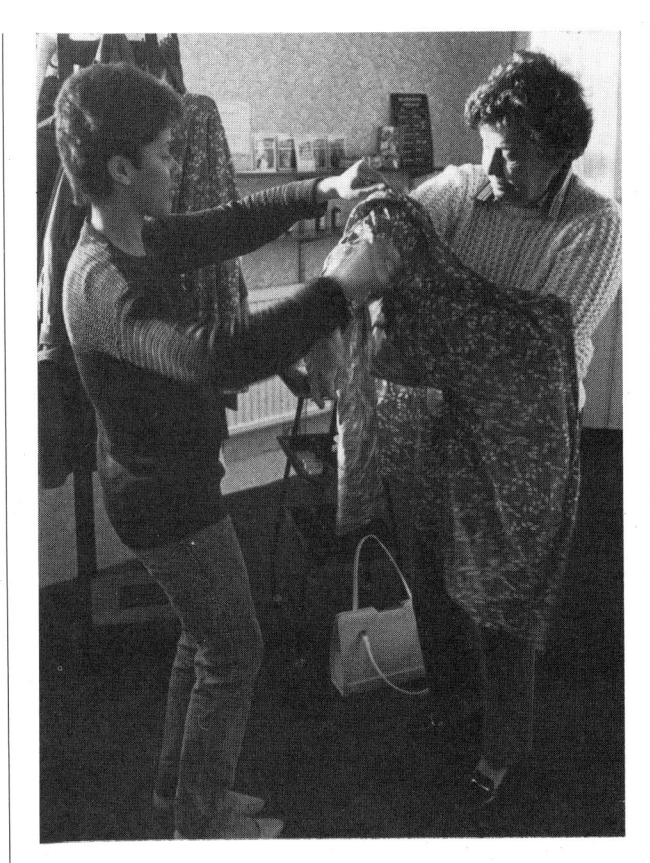

Above *Ismay helps a customer into a protective overall before starting on her hair.*

Below *Before styling or cutting, Ismay washes a customer's hair.*

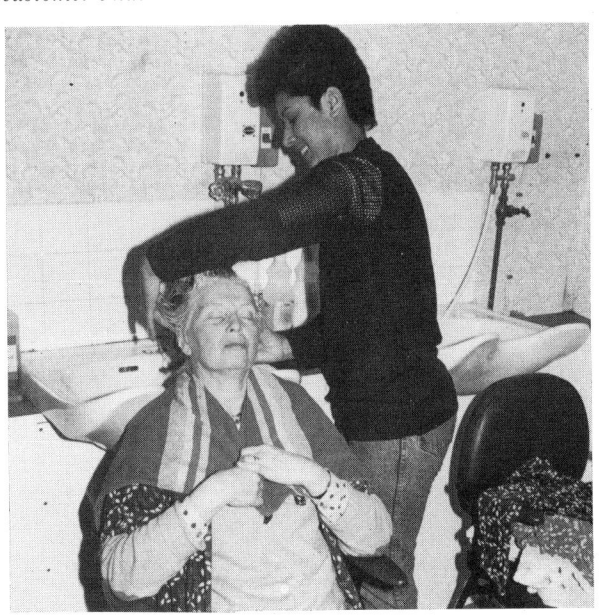

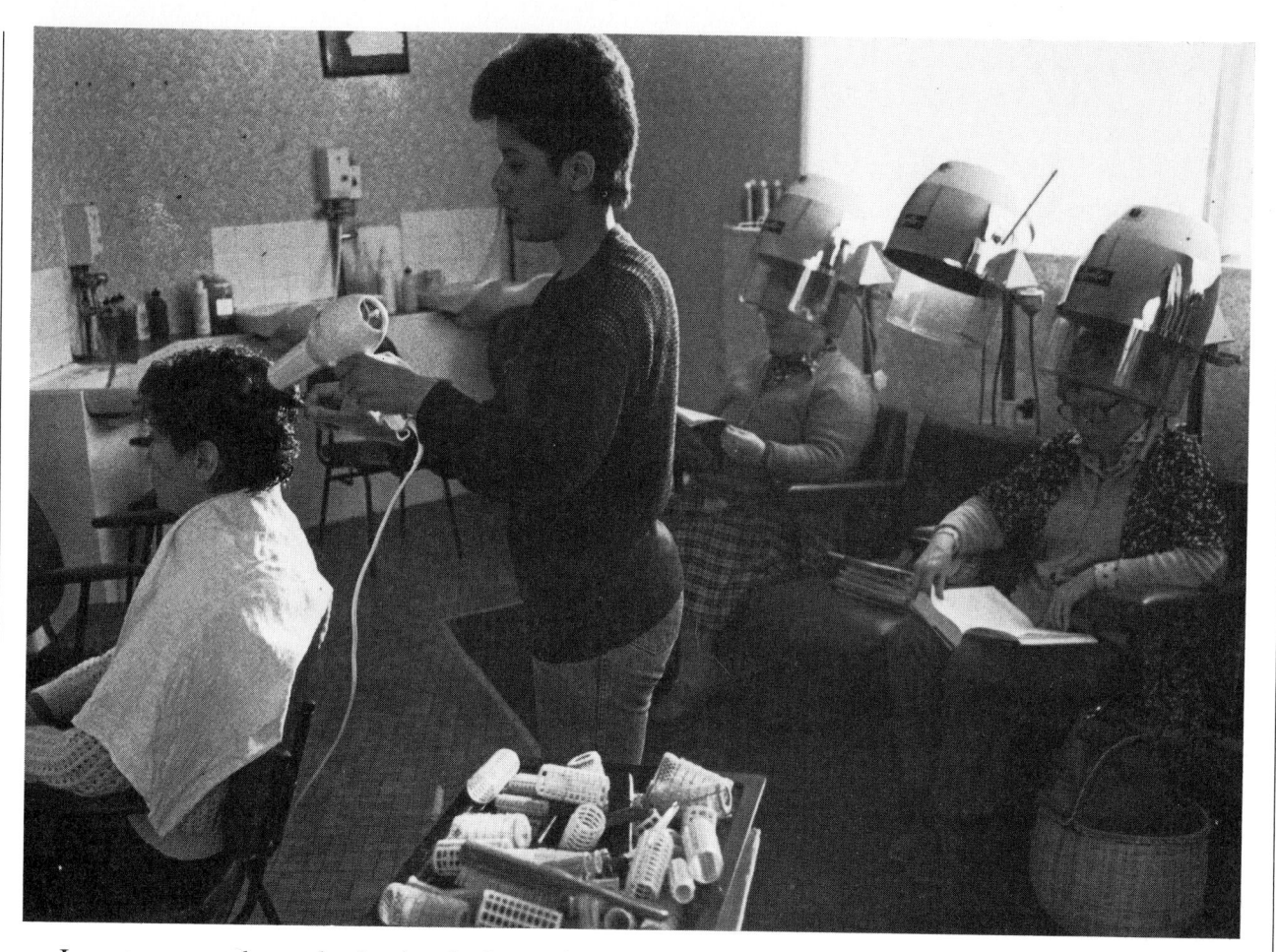

Ismay blow-dries a customer's hair, while two others wait under the large driers.

I cost my work on the basis of what other local salons are charging. My charges have increased considerably since I took over the business, and I make a good living, but if I started to charge too much, I would soon lose customers.

Each week, I buy a National Insurance stamp from the village post office, and put my takings into the bank. I don't have a separate personal account, so I deduct my own wages first. I have a deposit account for my savings. I give my records and receipts to the accountant who handles my tax affairs, and he gets in touch with me if there are any problems. To reduce my tax bill, I can claim many expenses, including my rent and rates, car, telephone, materials and equipment costs, working clothes and advertising.

I advertise in a magazine called *Sussex Life* and our parish magazine, but it's not really necessary because I'm now well known. I keep a stock of business cards by the door, so that customers can easily find my phone number, or pass it on to their friends. I keep my appointments book near the phone, because that's how I take almost all of my bookings.

I live above the salon, but when I finish work, I manage to 'switch off' as I close the door behind me and go upstairs. Last year, I tried to have a week off, but customers kept phoning up and I ended up working most of the time! I do manage to have the occasional day off, though, and I'm only open in the morning on Saturdays. This year I hope to have a holiday, and perhaps a friend will be able to look after the salon.

Most of my income is ploughed back into the business. A condition of my lease is that I redecorate the premises every four years. I want to do that soon, and it will cost a fair amount of money. Then there are my overheads, which are quite high: employer's liability insurance to cover my two part-time girls; insurance for the salon's large windows; life insurance for myself (a condition of the lease); heating (oil for the central heating system costs me about £400 a year); electricity, rent and rates. So I have to make sure that my profits are high enough to cover all these.

I find my job satisfying because it's creative, and I enjoy the contact with people. No two heads of hair are the same, which makes the work very varied, and I like the independence of working for myself. It gives me a good feeling inside when someone comes in looking untidy and walks out of the door looking really smart. If a customer is going out to a special function, and I've done a good job on their hair, it boosts their confidence and makes me feel that I've contributed something to the occasion.

A couple of my friends are hairdressers, but they work entirely from home, visiting their customer's houses. That way you need your own transport, but you cut down on all the other overheads. They can get away with the minimum of equipment, can afford to charge less, and have no outlay of capital. It's a good way for someone with experience of the job to set up on their own, but you still have to be prepared to work hard, and keep your accounts in good order. I bought a book about self-employment before I started, and read all the available leaflets which, together with my business course, made life a lot easier.

Ismay takes change from her cash drawer as she is paid by yet another satisfied customer.

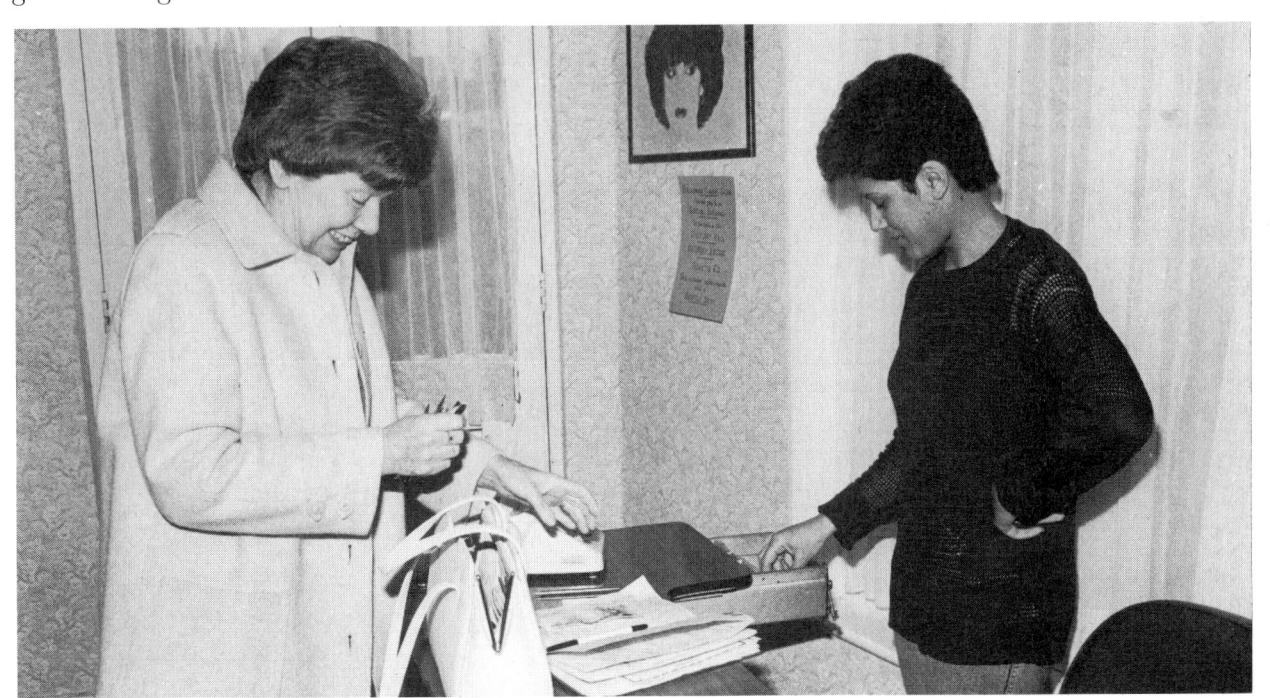

Bob Philpott
Mechanic

Bob Philpott is 29, and became a self-employed motorbike mechanic in 1982. He has a good reputation for a high standard of workmanship, and customers travel miles to have their bikes serviced by him. His business has now outgrown his back-garden workshop, so Bob is looking for larger premises.

I went to a local county secondary school. I left as soon as possible, when I was 16, with no qualifications at all. I was only good at woodwork, metalwork and engineering, but only on the practical side – I was never any good at putting things down on paper.

I knew at the time that I wanted to work with bikes, but there were no local openings for a trainee. So I went to work in a little factory making laboratory instruments. I gained some valuable experience there in working with sheet metal, but there was no real future in the job, and I left after nine months.

The manager of a local motorbike shop knew me fairly well, because I'd often bought spare-parts from him, and I asked him for a job. He knew that I already had an idea of the basics from working on friends' machines, and he offered me a job in his workshop.

I was very nervous at first, but I soon settled down and started picking up the basic skills, although I'm still learning every day – no one can know everything in this job. There weren't any training courses then for motorbike mechanics, but I don't think I've missed out. Practical experience is the best way to learn, although some formal training might have saved me time on some jobs.

I stayed in the workshop for six years before moving to another one as foreman. I enjoyed my work and would happily have stayed there, but the company was taken over, and I didn't like the new bosses. I left, and worked for a year in two other places before deciding to go it alone. I was already doing more and more private work in my spare time, and many customers had followed me around from job to job, so I had to make a decision. I'd thought before about setting up on my own, but I'd never had the courage to take the big step. I've a family to support, and a mortgage to pay off on my house, and I'd always been worried about earning enough

Bob is trying to trace a fault in the engine of a large Japanese motorbike.

To help him with any problems, Bob has a large collection of motorbike-repair manuals.

money without a regular job. My only regret now is not having made the decision earlier, before I had so many commitments.

It was very nerve-racking to begin with, because I wasn't sure how things would work out. I set up a workshop in the garage in my back garden, and placed a big advert in the local paper. I was amazed at the response, and stopped advertising after five months, because I couldn't cope with all the extra work. I didn't realize how many people knew my name from my previous jobs, and I soon had customers coming from as far away as London, Winchester and Brighton. Bike owners usually love their machines, and they appreciated the personal attention which I gave them.

49

I always work to a high standard on every job. I don't see the point of doing a job unless it's done properly. Also my rates are very reasonable; garages charge from £10 to £12 an hour for labour, whereas I only charge £7, because my overheads are lower. And I don't have to charge VAT because my annual turnover is less than £18,000. When I do become VAT registered, I shall have to add 15 per cent to my labour charges, but in return I'll be able to claim back any VAT which I pay during the year.

Bob's high standards of workmanship attract customers from far and wide.

When I first started, I soon discovered how useful a good accountant can be. My first one wasn't very helpful, but now I use an accountant who specializes in tax affairs for the self-employed. He saves me an awful lot of money, and has become a friend and adviser.

I had to move banks three times before I found an understanding bank manager. He has been very helpful, too, because I had no savings when I started, and I needed an overdraft to buy some special tools and to see me through the first few months.

I had some duplicate invoices printed with my address and telephone number, which is a good form of advertising, as well as providing the customer and myself with a clear record of what work I did and how much I charged. My wife, Jane, types them out and does the bookkeeping, when she's not busy looking after our two young children. I also give at least two of my business cards to every customer, which is another cheap and effective way of advertising your services.

After some initial cash-flow problems, the business has now progressed very well, and my only real problem is finding suitable premises. The workshop in the back garden was just a way of getting started, and I've now outgrown it. The council has refused to give me Light Industrial Permission, because the garage is in an unsuitable residential area. I don't really like working from home anyway, because people tend to phone and turn up at all hours, and it's impossible to ever leave work. I recently had a chap turn up at 11.30 p.m. with a puncture. Once I've found some suitable premises, I'd like to set up a proper breakdown-recovery service, and take on an apprentice to help out.

I get up at 7.00 a.m. and have breakfast with the family, before making out a list of the parts I need for the day's work. Jane usually collects these after taking our son to school. A

These four mercury gauges show the separate vacuums in each of the engine's carburretors.

car is essential (ours does thousands of miles every year) because the parts have to be collected from several different suppliers, depending on which make of bike I'm working on. I get a trade discount of between 15 and 20 per cent on spare parts, which helps to keep costs down.

I usually start work at about 9.00 a.m. I finish any time between 5 and 10 p.m., depending on how much work I have. I work on Saturdays, and sometimes on Sundays – if you want to build up your business you have to be prepared to sacrifice your spare time.

Customer relations is a very important aspect of the job, and I always give clients as much time as they want when they come in with a problem.

I had a good basic set of tools when I started, but I've still had to buy a lot more – last year I spent £3,000 on them alone. There are three different systems of spanners – metric, A.F. and Whitworth – and some makes of bike use all three, so I have a complete set of each. Large bikes are very heavy, so I use a hydraulic ramp to lift them to a sensible working height – I was lucky enough to buy one from a garage which had gone out of business. I use a compressor to work an airgun and for inflating tyres, and I have several special gauges for measuring such things as engine compression and carburettor vacuum. The welding set comes in very useful, and I also have several drills and grinders. Bike designs are advancing all the time, so buying tools is a never-ending process, but if you buy good quality tools and look after them, they'll pay for themselves many times over.

I hate having to ask for money more than once, and chasing debts used to be a real problem. I've just been paid for a job which I did five months ago, which means that all the profit has already been absorbed by interest charges on my overdraft. When we first started we had £1,000 of bounced cheques in one week, but things have fortunately improved since then!

I should buy my National Insurance stamps every week, but I tend to forget, and it soon mounts up to a sizeable sum. I'm going

Below *Building a wheel by hand is a very skilled job, but it is all in a day's work for Bob.*

Bob checks the tyre pressures.

to arrange to pay my contributions on a standing order at the bank, which is a fairly 'painless' way of doing things. I don't have a separate business account yet, but I keep a careful record of all my income and expenses. I don't pay myself a set wage, but all my profits are either ploughed back into the business or spent on renovating our house.

I feel it's better to spend money on tools and materials rather than giving it to the taxman, and my claimable expenses in the first year were so high that I only paid £220 in tax. We haven't had a holiday for three years, but this year we're hoping to go to Cornwall or Wales for a week or so. The trouble is that the summer is my busiest time, so perhaps a winter holiday would be the best idea.

Rosalind Nice
Caterer

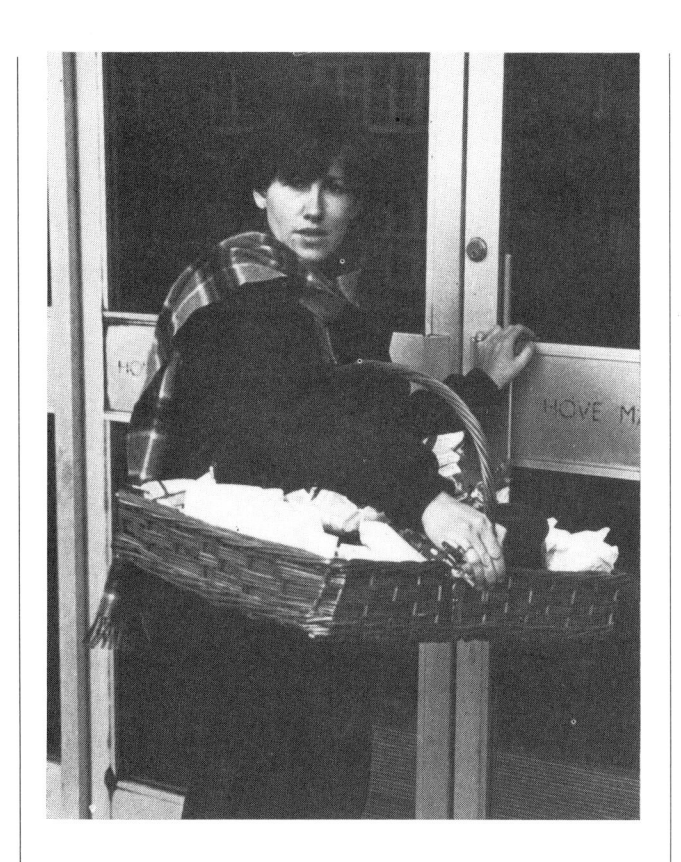

Rosalind Nice's experience provides a perfect example of how a good idea can be turned into a thriving business. Every morning, she and her helpers drive around the Brighton area, delivering sandwiches and drinks to firms. She started the business two years ago, and managed to survive a shaky beginning, through perseverance and enthusiasm. Now 27 years old, she is about to open a restaurant.

Most workers eat the same boring sandwiches day after day, but I aim to change all that and bring some fun and variety into their diet with my range of 'superior sandwiches'. This week's menu, for example, offers 'Calcutta', filled with curried egg mayonnaise, mango chutney and salad; and 'Miss Piggy', filled with honey-roast ham and home-made coleslaw. Many customers were very conservative in their tastes at first, and reluctant to try my more 'exotic' sandwiches, but now they'll eat anything, and eagerly wait to see the new menu each week!

When I left school at 16, I never dreamed that I would work in the food trade, and had no interest in cooking at all. I went to a private school, and art was always my best subject and main interest. I had 4 'O' levels and art 'A' level, and wanted to go to art college, with the aim of being a book illustrator.

At first, I worked in a nursery school, but then I saw an advert in the local paper for thin people to work as film extras. I put on my tightest clothes, went for an interview, and was accepted – as a concentration camp inmate! For two months, I had to wear rags and clogs, with dirty hair and open sores on my face – all for a few seconds' appearance on the finished film. But it was great fun, and the money I earned paid for trips to Paris and Greece.

Art college, though, was a real disappointment. The travelling took two hours each way, and I soon became disillusioned, because my heart wasn't in it. I realized that I'd never make an artist, and I left before the end of the foundation year. I still sketch and paint whenever I have time, and I do sometimes regret not finishing the course.

My Mum persuaded me to go in for secretarial work, and I passed my typing and shorthand exams at the end of a six-month course. I worked for a year as a secretary with a large electronics firms, but found it pretty boring. A friend told me about a cordon bleu cookery course in London, which she said was great fun, so I decided to try it. My Mum paid the fees for the three-month course, but I had to use my own savings for living expenses, which in London are very high.

Rosalind has to be fit to carry her heavily laden basket from customer to customer.

Although I knew nothing about cookery beforehand, I really enjoyed the course, and the tutors had us cooking from the very first day. It was during the heatwave of 1976, though, and the temperature in the kitchens was over 38°C (100°F). It was impossible to make some things, like pastry, because butter and fat just melted as soon as they were taken out of the fridge. It was hard work, but it taught me to do everything by hand, using only the finest ingredients.

Afterwards, I was interviewed for several catering jobs in Brighton, but they all offered very poor wages. I had a few private catering jobs, cooking for dinner parties and the like, but not enough to provide a real income. My Mum ran a nursing home, and when her cook left, she offered me the job. It was very good experience for me, and good for her too – hers was the only home in the Yellow Pages offering cordon bleu cooking! It was very demanding as I had to buy all the food and cook at least three meals a day, sometimes catering for special diets, but I enjoyed it. I was very adventurous in my cooking, and the old people loved it.

In 1981, my mother decided to retire, and I thought it was time to start my own business. I heard about a firm in London which was selling home-made sandwiches to office workers, and I could see that the idea had great potential in an area like Brighton. I didn't have the courage to do it on my own, and persuaded a friend to be my business partner.

We spent about £100 on food, paper bags, baskets and uniforms, because at first we used to dress as maids. I hated the uniforms, but it certainly worked as a publicity gimmick because we were on the front page of the local newspaper on our first day. We also had signs made for our cars, but didn't bother with any other advertising – personal introductions are the best way of getting business, I've found.

Above *One of Rosalind's regular customers is a motor-accessory shop.*

We started on my birthday. I was a nervous wreck, and the first day was an absolute disaster! We had put hand-printed green labels inside the food bags, and it wasn't until the end of the morning that we discovered that the green ink was running on to the sandwiches! We were lucky, because the next day I only found one company who had bought green sandwiches. They were furious, but were quite happy when I gave them all a free sandwich.

It was very difficult building up the business at first, and regular customers were few and far between. I found it best to approach the manager – usually with a free sample – when canvassing for business, and sales gradually started to improve. My partner, though, who was married and had children, didn't have the time to give the same commitment to the business, and she pulled out after three months. I wanted to earn a good living, and was prepared to sacrifice all my time and energy.

As she arrives at each customer, Rosalind re-stocks her basket from boxes in the back of her car.

An office-worker reads Rosalind's new menu before choosing. The menu is changed every week for variety.

The customers can't see what they're buying, because of the special bags which I use, so the menu is very important. I try to think up amusing and eye-catching names for my different sandwich recipes, and I make the menu as varied as possible, to appeal to a wide range of tastes. People often pin the menus on their wall, and have decided what they want even before I arrive. Changing the menu each week is important, and it gives me a good excuse to return to any company which turned me down before!

Things are now going very well, and I usually serve about 100 customers each morning. The weather affects sales, though: if it's too cold, people want a hot meal, and they lose their appetites if it's too hot. Wet days are best, because they don't want to go out in the rain to buy food.

I can't manage on my own any longer, and I have two girls to help me to prepare and deliver the food. I give them a commission and a basic wage, and pay their petrol expenses, but they have to provide their own transport.

My day starts at 7.00 a.m., when I have a cup of coffee and begin making the sandwiches. I now have a food processor, which is wonderful for grating and slicing cheese and vegetables, and I use a slicer for bread and meat. I quickly wrap the sandwiches and load the baskets, ready to go into the back of the car. As well as sandwiches, I also sell crisps, chocolate, buttered buns, rolls and fruit juices. Some companies phone me with their orders, which is very helpful.

At 10.00 a.m., I meet the girls, give them their baskets, and we start on our rounds. It's important to get around as quickly as you can, because no one is interested in buying anything after 1 p.m., and whatever you have left is wasted. On the way home, I go to a local bakery which bakes its own delicious bread on the premises. Good bread is very important, and I buy a selection of loaves, French sticks, buns and rolls – about £50 worth each week. I buy my vegetables from the market, because they're cheaper and of higher quality, and my meat comes from a very good local butcher. Once a week I visit a wholesaler to buy my crisps, fruit juice and chocolate. Good-quality ingredients are very important, and it's surprising how much you can save by shopping around.

When I've finished shopping, I come home and do some preparation for the next day, such as making coleslaw and mayonnaise, before cleaning the work surfaces. Hygiene is very important when handling food. When I first started, I informed the council's health department and they sometimes send inspectors to check my kitchen. Just in case I do accidentally poison someone, I'm insured with a public liability policy, which costs about £30 a year. I also have another policy which will pay me a disability allowance if I'm forced to stop work because of an injury.

With the help of a bank overdraft, I recently bought a shop which I'm turning into a restaurant, and that takes up a lot of my time. I also occasionally cater for dinner parties, directors' business luncheons, and other private functions, so I'm kept fairly busy most of the time.

When working out my prices, I have to keep a careful eye on my costs for materials, petrol, wages and fuel bills, because it's very easy not to make any profit for all your hard work. Although I'm now doing well, I still don't earn enough for all the work I put into the business, but at least I'm working for myself, and I refuse even to contemplate being a failure.

On her way home, Rosalind drops into a baker to buy her next day's supply of bread. Here she is paying for it.

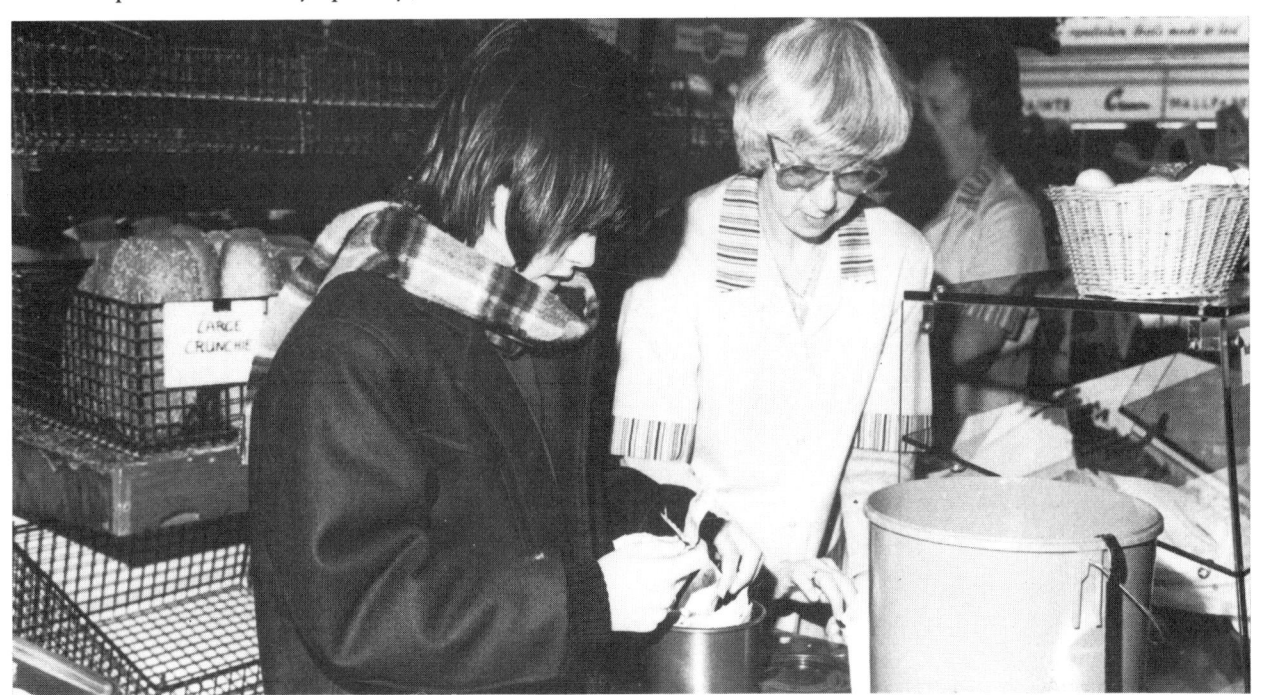

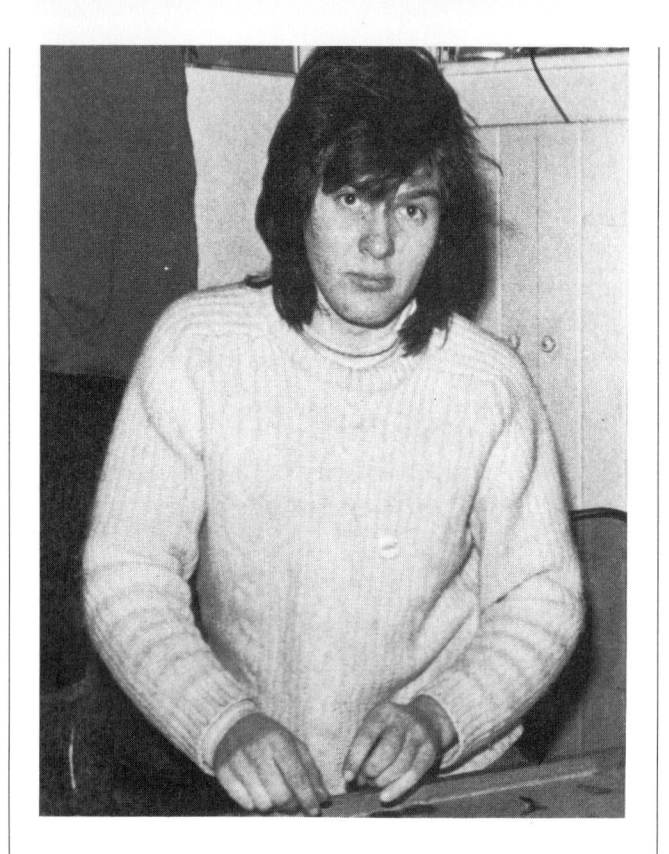

Edgar Symes
Glass craftsman

Edgar Symes is 22 years old, and has been a self-employed glass craftsman since 1981. As well as making and repairing leaded windows, he designs and constructs terrariums and lampshades. So far, Edgar has deliberately kept his business small, but plans to expand it by advertising.

I never used to be interested in glass, and started working with it more or less by accident. But now it's a real passion. To see my original flat designs on paper transformed by the magical combination of glass and light, setting off the colours against each other, it's like music to the eye!

My father and three of my four brothers are tree surgeons, but I've never had any desire to follow them into the 'family business'. I went to a local comprehensive, and left when I was 16 with four 'O' levels, including woodwork, and CSEs in maths and technical drawing. I then moved on to a sixth form college, but they were using a new streaming system which was totally chaotic. After one very dissatisfied year, I decided to leave and find a job.

While at school, I used to earn extra pocket money by doing gardening at weekends. When I left, I had no real idea of what I wanted to do. I had a vague romantic notion of working on a game reserve in Africa, but ended up as a gardener in Sussex! My Dad knew the owners of a large well-kept private garden and he arranged a meeting with them. I had no qualifications or references, but they took me on right away. They were very good employers, and I enjoyed being outside and working with plants. I was very happy there for eighteen months, but then I began to feel isolated, as I worked on my own most of the time, and I realized that there was no real future in the job.

At about the same time a friend of mine, who worked in a glass workshop, decided to emigrate, and he asked if I would like to take over his job. I went to the workshop to see what was involved, and had a chat with the boss. There was no formal interview, but he agreed to take me on for a trial period of a few months. I found it strange at first, working with a new person, in a new environment and with new materials, but it was also exciting. What started as a change, and a novelty, soon turned into a real passion as I became more experienced, and began to appreciate the real beauty of glass.

I started off making terrariums, which are leaded-glass plant containers of different sizes and shapes, sometimes with patterns in coloured glass. As my skills developed, I moved on to more complicated projects – opalescent-glass lampshades, leaded lights, and special commissions in coloured and stained glass. My boss became a good friend, and I think he kept me on because I showed an affinity with craft work. I didn't mind working unusual hours, and he was pleased with my standards of workmanship.

After about two years, though, demand began to fall off and the workshop wasn't providing enough money for his family to live on. So, he emigrated to Silicon Valley in California to work on computers, and the workshop closed down. I bought his tools and stock of materials, and decided to go it alone. I couldn't work for the first few months because I had no premises.

Eventually a friend, who runs a local organic farm, offered me the use of her old farm shop, which was being used as a tool shed. I cleaned it out, plugged a few leaks in the roof, installed a paraffin heater and some carpet, and set to work. My boss had left me his old order book. Although now a few months out of date, I phoned some people in it and was offered several repair jobs, mainly on front doors with damaged Victorian stained-glass panels. It was a good beginning because my workshop was still not fully functional, and most of these jobs could be done *in situ*.

During slack periods, I started using the workshop to build up a stock of terrariums, ornamental glass boxes and hanging glass

Above *Edgar sorts out pieces of coloured glass to use in a large window.*

Below *Edgar gives a final polish to the window which he gave his parents for a wedding anniversary.*

plaques, which I took around to local craft shops to be sold a on 'sale or return' basis. I have never advertised my products or services, but I get a fairly steady flow of work from word of mouth. If things are very quiet, I sometimes bolster up my income by doing gardening or odd-jobs. I still have all the contacts from the original business to set up an export trade if I ever want to, but at the moment I'm content to rely on the local market. We once sold a terrarium to the Botanical Gardens in New York, and perhaps I'll follow that one up one day.

Edgar cleans the putty from the edges of a leaded-glass window which he has made and installed.

I'm officially classified as a 'low-earner', but because of my circumstances I don't really need to earn a lot of money. I live on an estate in a tied cottage. Instead of paying rent, I work two days a week on the estate as a gardener and handyman. It's not an ideal arrangement because it cuts down my effective working week, but it does mean that I don't have to worry about finding the rent money. I have a similar arrangement with the farmer who owns my workshop. She's a friend, and I make her leaded windows and ornamental hanging designs, showing her farm produce, instead of paying rent. Between friends, I feel that swapping services is much better than exchanging cash.

All the materials for my craft are very expensive – a fact that isn't always appreciated by customers. I have to go to London to buy all the glass from a specialist firm which sells glass of every thickness, colour and texture, including handblown and handrolled glass – their range really is enormous. The lead comes from another London firm, and I buy it in bundles of long strips of different widths. In spite of trade discounts, solder, copper tape and chemicals are also expensive, and maintaining a reasonable profit margin on my products is sometimes very difficult. I'm improving all the time in my techniques, and I can work faster than I used to, but speed isn't essential. I always put quality before quantity, but quality is something which people should be prepared to pay for!

Costing a job is always difficult, and I don't really think that I get a fair return for my time and effort. Customers sometimes don't appreciate the skills involved in the work, or the high cost of my materials. But I've never had any problems over payment – in fact some customers have complained that my prices were too low, and paid me extra! It's a nice gesture, and very rewarding when it happens. I often get repeat orders from past customers, which is always very pleasing.

The tools which I use for my craft are fairly specialized, so they do tend to be expensive. I use a heavy-duty soldering iron with an inbuilt thermostat, so that it heats and melts

In a local craft shop, Edgar sees a place in the window to hang his terrarium.

When he has made a terrarium, Edgar checks that it doesn't leak by pouring a glass of water into it.

the solder, but not the lead! The solder which I use is 60 per cent tin and 40 per cent silver, so it's expensive too. Some people use a diamond-tipped glass-cutter, which is good for certain cuts and kinds of glass, but I prefer to use one with replaceable tungsten wheels. I've tried many tools for scraping off excess putty, but nothing beats the French lobster pick which I 'inherited' from the previous business. I also use various special pliers.

I made my own light-box, which is an important piece of equipment. After cutting a hole in my work bench, I covered it with a sheet of clear plate glass, and underneath I tacked a foil-lined box with a light bulb inside. I mainly use it for seeing the template when I'm cutting dark-coloured or opalescent glass.

Because my whole family is self-employed, we all use the same accountant. His services are very useful, when filling out tax returns. I keep all my receipts for materials, petrol, telephone, and heating, and these all help to keep my tax bill down. I have a building society account for current expenditure on bills and materials, and a bank deposit account for my personal savings.

There are a few things about this job which I don't enjoy, such as starting work in a cold workshop. In fact, I don't usually start until late morning, and then I work late into the evening. I prefer working these hours, and the radio programmes are usually better in the evening! Glass never looks its best unless it is spotlessly clean, but I don't really like doing it. Sometimes it can take ages, because the soldering flux leaves a hard smear on the glass, which can be very hard to remove.

Being self-employed is ideal for me, because I'm obligated to no one but myself; I'm my own boss and I work the hours that suit me. I enjoy working with my hands, designing my own work, and I usually like the things I make.

Mark Burlington
Gardener

Mark Burlington, 27, worked for several years in offices and with handicapped children before deciding that he wanted a complete change. With a minimum of experience, no tools, and only a bicycle for transport, he advertised his services as a jobbing gardener, and soon had as much work as he could handle.

I'll never make a fortune from gardening, but money isn't the main thing in my life. It's easy to set up as a gardener, and it's a healthy, satisfying way of life which does provide me with a fairly good living. I enjoy being in the open air, and the variety of work that this job brings.

I went to a fee-paying grammar school in Sussex, but I'd had enough of the school environment by the age of 16 and wanted to get out, so I left with 5 'O' levels. I found a job doing clerical work for the local council; but I didn't really like being cooped up in an office, doing the same thing day after day, and I left after three years.

I then worked for two and a half years as a class helper at a centre for physically and mentally handicapped children. It was fantastic! I found it very satisfying helping these children to develop, and I decided to take some formal training. I started a three-year course for teaching the handicapped at Twickenham Teacher Training College, but took the second year off to go to America. There I helped out with a schools' theatre project and travelled around, but I came back too late to continue my course.

I wanted a complete break from working with children, so I moved to London and worked as a gardener in a large park, which is where my interest in gardening started. I enjoyed the outdoor life, and spent my time digging, mowing lawns and pruning shrubs, learning all the basic gardening skills. It was only a temporary summer job, and afterwards I worked at a variety of things before deciding to leave the big city and move back to Sussex.

It was very difficult to find a job, and I ended up as a labourer on a building site, but was laid off after six months. By then, I'd had enough of working to a routine, and taking orders from someone else, so I decided to set up on my own.

I decided on gardening partly because it doesn't need a lot of money to get started. I put lots of cards in local shop windows, and placed an advert in the local newspaper for two weeks, offering regular garden maintenance. The response was very good – it certainly provided enough customers to get started. I stipulated that the customer should provide all tools, which saved a lot of expense, and for the first nine months I used a bicycle to travel from job to job. I soon became very fit, because apart from the gardening, I was cycling up to ten miles to each customer!

I didn't have much experience when I first started, three years ago, and I often had to use books, feeling my way as I went along. I did make a few blunders at first, such as pulling up shrubs instead of weeds, but I improved with experience. I found it difficult to work out prices for jobs, but after talking to other jobbing gardeners, I based my charges on a £2 hourly rate. It provided an adequate income from the start, although I have increased my charges since then, and now tend to charge according to the amount of work involved.

After the first two weeks, I never had to advertise, and I now get all my work from personal recommendation from my regular customers. I do have occasional 'one-offs', but most of my customers are regular, and I pay weekly visits to about 15 or 20 of them. I live in a good area, because there are plenty of houses with very large gardens and grounds, which need constant maintenance to keep

Garden maintenance involves many jobs – such as mending broken fences.

Mark checks the oil level in the motor mower before he starts to mow the lawn.

them looking tidy and attractive.

I usually get up early and have a large breakfast, which is important if you're doing a physical job in the open air. I now have a van, and a few tools, so I load them before driving to my first garden. I usually start work at 8.30 a.m. I never work less than two hours at any one place, although it can be as long as eight hours in the summer. When I've finished at one house, I drive to the next and start immediately, not usually bothering to stop for lunch.

The work is varied, and includes hedge-cutting, making bonfires, digging, weeding, and general tidying. Some of my customers are old ladies who can't get out to do their own shopping, so I often do that for them as well. If the weather is too bad to work outside, I sometimes get asked to do some painting, or odd-jobs around the house. I work longer hours in summer, because there is more to do in the gardens, and more hours of daylight. Customers with large gardens keep me on during the winter, but there is usually nothing to do in the smaller ones.

I have to try to earn enough in the busy summer months to see me through the quiet winter periods. Sometimes in the winter the weather is so bad that I can't work at all, but I don't really mind, because I have plenty of other interests to keep me busy.

Some customers have specific things which they want me to do, while others leave it up to me to choose, but I come into contact with them on almost every visit. It's very important to get on well with them all, and I've always tried to be polite and helpful from the very start. Now I know them all, and their families, and they are all pretty friendly, and usually come out with a welcome cup of tea. If they are out, they trust me enough to leave the keys for me, but it wasn't always like that to start with. I've had some awkward customers

Above *Mark prunes a climbing rose – a time-consuming job.*

Mark piles logs after chopping them up. He has become very fit in the last few years!

who were impossible to please, but I've always managed to drop them as I've found new people.

I like the variety of working in different gardens and doing different jobs every day, and the flexibility of the work gives me the chance to take time off for other things when I want to. In wet weather, I sometimes get really soaked, which isn't much fun, but it's one of the few disadvantages of the job.

I share a house with friends, and our telephone is very important. Customers often phone me with instructions, or to tell me that they're going away, and I can get in touch with them if I'm ill, or want to change my arrangements.

I'm paid daily, in cash, for my work. I pay some of it into a current bank account to cover bills, and I have a deposit account to save for holidays and the like. Apart from rent and petrol, I don't have many expenses, and my finances are fairly simple. I buy National Insurance stamps every week, and an accountant helps me to work out my small tax bill.

Digging over flower-beds takes up a lot of Mark's time in the winter months.

After he has mown the lawn, Mark finishes the job with these edging shears.

I have bought some tools, such as my electric hedge-clipper, to make my work easier, and I have learnt many new gardening skills, but I've no great ambition to expand my business. As I charge by the hour, there's no point trying to work faster to earn more money, and I don't have to hurry my jobs. I could easily employ someone else, and invest some money in mowers and other machinery, but I'm not really interested – I'm happy as I am. I'm not after a lot of money, and I value my free time too much to become a slave to my job. I only work to live, rather than living to work!

How to Become Self-Employed

As you can see from the experiences of the people featured in this book, these are both advantages and disadvantages to being self-employed. Hard work and long hours are usually needed in return for the freedom and satisfaction of working for yourself.

The self-employed have to look after their own National Insurance and tax affairs, which usually involves a lot of tiresome paperwork; but they can claim most of their business costs as tax-allowable expenses.

The benefits available to most employees of firms – such as sick pay, paid holidays and company pensions – are denied to the self-employed, who have to make their own arrangements.

Everyone's needs vary, but there are certain points which should be helpful to anyone who is considering setting up their own business.

First, think carefully about your scheme, and research the possible market for the product or service which you intend to sell. Talk to as many people as possible who work in the same field, to build up your initial contacts and to save making obvious mistakes. Your local Citizens' Advice Bureau (listed in your local telephone directory) will be able to give you general advice and point you in the right direction for more information.

Try to save enough money to buy equipment and materials, and to tide you over the first few difficult months of your new venture. If you are unsure about handling money and book-keeping, enrol on an evening course, and visit your local reference library to learn all you can. It is essential to keep your accounts' books straight from the very start.

Contact your local tax office (listed under Inland Revenue in your local telephone directory) and inform them that you intend to start self-employment. Failure to do this can result in a hefty and crippling tax bill in the future. You will have to declare your income for tax purposes at the end of the financial year, and this is where a good accountant is invaluable.

It makes good sense to open a business account at your bank, to keep your personal and business finances separate. An understanding bank manager will also grant loan or overdraft facilities, to buy new equipment and overcome temporary cash-flow problems. Most bank managers are also a valuable source of general and business information.

Your local Jobcentre (listed in your local telephone directory) and Department of Health and Social Security office (listed in your local telephone directory under Health and Social Security, Dept. of) will provide advisory leaflets on all aspects of self-employment, and a National Insurance card, on which to stick your weekly contribution stamps. The stamps are available from post offices, but a direct debit payment from your bank account is probably the most convenient way to pay your contributions.

Some self-employed workers need special insurance cover, such as public liability policies, to protect them if they cause damage to others or their property, in the course of their work. Because there is no sick-pay scheme, it makes good sense to take out a disability policy in case you are prevented from working through an accident or illness. Life insurance and a pension scheme are also advisable, and a good insurance broker can help with this.

Since 1983, the Manpower Services Commission has provided places for 25,000 previously unemployed people on the Enterprise Allowance Scheme. Applicants have to possess £1,000 to invest in their business, and gain approval for their idea; in return, they are paid £40 a week for their first year of business, to help get their venture off the ground.

Some areas of self-employment – building or working with food, for example – involve the consent of local authority bodies, including health and planning departments, so the services of a solicitor may be necessary.

Being self-employed usually involves *selling* something, whether it be your talents, your services, or your products. To reach all your potential clients, some form of advertising (business cards, adverts in local newspapers, door-to-door leaflets, etc.) is usually a good investment, but not as good as word-of-mouth recommendations from satisfied customers. An ability to get on with people, and to be cheerful and friendly, is a great asset. Determination, enthusiasm and optimism are also necessary in the early months, which can be very difficult. Deciding to go into business on your own is a big step, so think about it carefully. But, if you are sure that it is what you want, then go ahead – and good luck!

Jobs for the Self-Employed

Accountant
Actor
Animal breeder
Antiques dealer
Antiques restorer
Architect
Artist
Beautician
Blacksmith
Builder
Carpenter
Carpet cleaner
Carpet layer
Caterer
Child-minder
Chimney sweep
Clothes-maker
Dentist
Designer
Disco D.J.
Doctor
Driving instructor
Electrician
Estate agent
Farmer
Fisherman
Gardener
Hairdresser
Illustrator
Jeweller
Journalist
Market-stall holder
Mechanic
Painter/Decorator
Photographer
Physiotherapist
Plumber
Potter
Printer
Publican
Salesman
Sculptor
Sign writer
Sportsman/woman
Taxi driver
Tree surgeon
Typist
Van driver
Upholsterer
Watchmaker
Weaver
Writer

Sources of Further Information

Small Firms Information Centre: Dail 100 for the operator and ask for Freephone 2444 for advice on any business problem.

National Federation of the Self-Employed
32 St Annes Road West
Lytham St Annes
Lancashire FY8 1NY

Association of Independent Businesses
Europe House
World Trade Centre
London E1 9AA

Small Firms Centre
8 Bulstrode Street
London W1M 7FT

Council for Small Industries in Rural Areas (CoSIRA)
141 Castle Street
Salisbury
Wiltshire SP1 3TP

Some Useful Books to Consult Are:

A Bit on the Side – How to Make Money by Working from Home by Christine Brady (Collins, 1983; £3.95)

Be Your Own Boss (National Extension College/Yorkshire TV, 1982; £5.95)

Start Your Own Business by Judy Hillman (London Enterprise Agency, 1982; £2.50)

The Sunday Times Self-Help Directory (Granada, 1982; £3.95)

Starting Your Own Business (Consumers' Association, 1983; £4.95)

Check Your Tax (W. Foulsham & Co. Ltd, annual publication; £1.25)

Work for Yourself – A Guide for Young People by Paddy Hall (National Extension College, 1983; £3.25)

The Small Business Guide by Colin Barrow (BBC, 1982; £4.50)

How to Start and Run Your Own Business by M. Mogano (Graham & Trotman, 1983; £3.95)

How to Set Up and Run Your Own Business (The Daily Telegraph, 1983; £2.95)

The Hambro Tax Guide by W. I. Sinclair (Oyez Longman, annual publication; £9.95)

Index

A

accidents 16, 37, 57
accountant 10, 22, 36, 42, 46, 50, 62, 66
advantages of self-employment 6, 12, 13, 20, 21, 23, 37, 47, 62, 63, 66
advertising 6, 11, 13, 14, 32, 33, 42, 46, 49, 50, 54, 60, 64

B

banks
    business account 9, 22, 35
    deposit account 46, 62, 66
    managers 9, 36, 37, 50
    overdrafts 9, 22, 33, 35, 50, 52, 57
book-keeping 10, 16, 35, 36, 37, 42, 43, 45, 46, 50, 62
building society account 17, 62
business cards 11, 46, 50

C

competition 12, 46
contacts 20, 22, 24, 25, 26, 27, 42, 59
customers
    awkward 65–6
    dealing with 16, 27, 35–6, 37, 45, 51, 61, 65
    payment from 17, 52, 61

D

disadvantages of self-employment 18, 20, 38, 41, 45, 51, 55, 62

E

educational qualifications
    'A' levels 13, 23, 33, 38, 53
    college of technology 8, 34, 43
    CSEs 8, 13, 23, 43, 58
    City & Guilds diplomas 8, 43
    night school 18, 43
    'O' levels 8, 13, 23, 33, 38, 53, 58, 63
    polytechnic 18, 33
    sixth form college 23
    university 18
Enterprise Allowance Scheme 7, 8–9
equipment
    cost of 9, 12, 13, 14, 33, 37, 42, 50, 51, 54, 57

H

holidays 7, 9, 22, 46–7, 52
hours of work 12, 13, 14, 17, 26, 30–31, 34–5, 42, 43, 44, 51, 56–7, 65

I

income 7, 17, 21, 27, 38, 41, 56
insecurity 20, 38, 41, 42, 48–9
insurance 14, 16, 22, 32, 37, 42, 47, 57
    cost of 16, 57

J

Jobcentre 6, 8, 24

L

labour rates 12, 14, 21, 32, 40, 46, 50, 57, 61, 64
legal action 41

M

market research 17, 27
Musicians' Union 40

N

National Federation of the Self-Employed 37
National Insurance stamps 9, 27, 32, 36, 42, 46, 52, 66
number of self-employed 6

O

overheads 9, 16, 32, 36, 37, 47, 50

P

pensions 7, 23, 37
Public Lending Right 21
public liability insurance 14, 16, 22, 32, 37, 57

R

reputation 19, 22, 33, 49, 64
royalty payments 21, 40

S

self-discipline 12, 37
Small Claims Court 41
Small Firms Service 9
specialist suppliers 12, 17, 45, 51, 61
sub-contracting 34, 56

69

T

tax 10, 17, 22, 27, 32, 42, 46, 50, 52, 62, 66
trade discount 17, 34, 45, 51, 61
trade magazines 45

V

Value Added Tax (VAT) 22, 36, 37, 50

W

wholesaler 57

Y

Youth Training Scheme 7, 34

Acknowledgements

The author and the publishers would like to thank all those who appear in this book, and the Kings Head Hotel, Cuckfield, for their co-operation.